SORRY GNAT SORRY
PEST CONTROL

MITE CLUB
EXTERMINATORS

BUGSHEAD
RE-SQUISHETED
PEST CONTROL

I0759752

BIG LITTLE FLIES
PEST CONTROL

THE EXOR-PEST
PEST CONTROL

Are You There Bug?
It's Me, Margaret
The Exterminator

THE YOUNG
AND THE PESTLESS

Slay Ride
EXTERMINATORS

BOOGIE MITES
EXTERMINATORS

Slay Anything
PEST CONTROL

You Should Get That
Mole Looked At
EXTERMINATORS

MUST BE
MICE!

WHEN YOU SQUISH
UPON A STAR

VERMIN ON THE VERGE
OF A
NERVOUS BEATDOWN
PEST CONTROL

THE
BEE-STING
BOYS

Killing Fleas Softly
(With Our Spray)
PEST CONTROL

DAZED AND
CON-FUMED

THE ANTS GO MARCHING
NONE BY NONE

TAKE A ANTS ON ME
EXTERMINATOR

BEETLES JUICED

TO KILL A
SHOCKING BUG
Exterminators

BUGS DONE-Y
PEST CONTROL

I ALWAYS FEEL LIKE
SOMEBODY'S SQUASHING ME
PEST CONTROL

LIKE DEAD BUGS
AND I CANNOT LIE
PEST CONTROL

THEY TERMITE BE
GIANTS
Exterminators

BEAST
INFECTION
PEST CONTROL

SHALL WE ANTS?
Exterminators

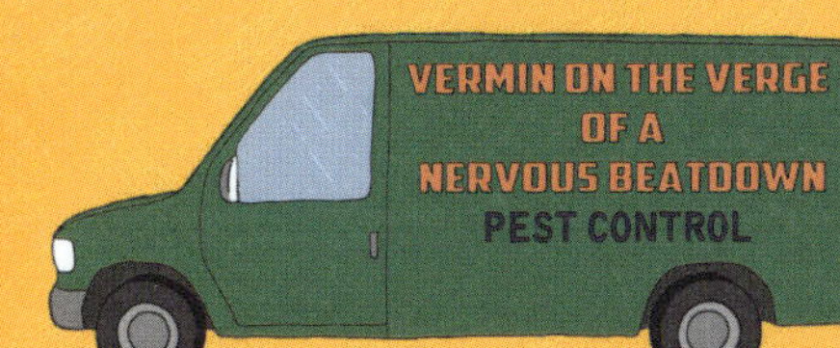

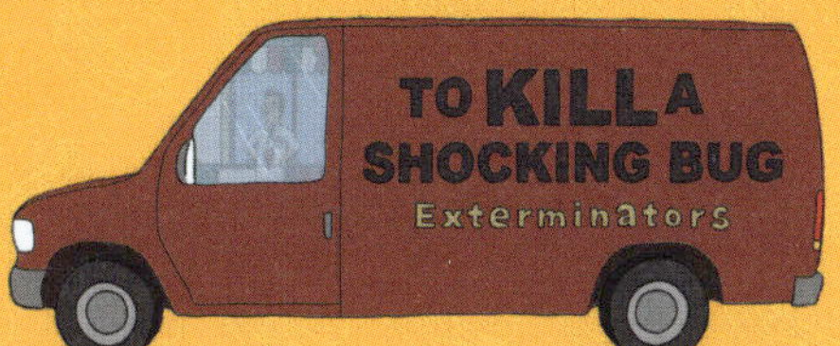

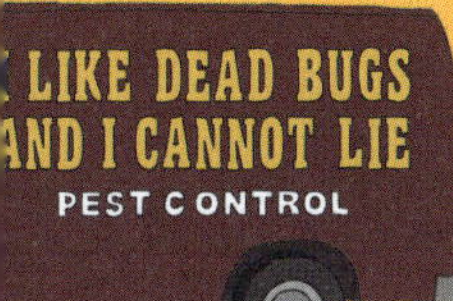

First published in the United States of America
in 2025 by
Rizzoli Universe
A Division of Rizzoli International Publications, Inc.
49 West 27th Street
New York, NY 10001
www.rizzoliusa.com

Bob's Burgers™ & © 20th Television 2025

For Bento Box:
Text: Loren Bouchard & Bernard Derriman
Creative Director: Bernard Derriman
Book Design: Michael Macasero &
Christopher Collard
Front & Back Cover: Phil Hayes &
Ruben Hickman

For Rizzoli:
Publisher: Charles Miers
Associate Publisher: Jessica Fuller
Editor: Jacob Lehman
Production Manager: Maria Pia Gramaglia
Managing Editor: Lynn Scrabis

All rights reserved. No part of this publication
may be reproduced, stored in a retrieval system, or
transmitted in any form or by any means, electronic,
mechanical, photocopying, recording, or otherwise,
without prior consent of the publishers.

Printed in Italy

Th e authorized representative in the EU for product
safety and compliance is Mondadori Libri S.p.A.,
via Gian Battista Vico 42, Milan, Italy, 20123.
www.mondadori.it

2025 2026 2027 2028 / 10 9 8 7 6 5 4 3 2
ISBN: 978-0-7893-4432-8
Library of Congress Control Number: 2025934701

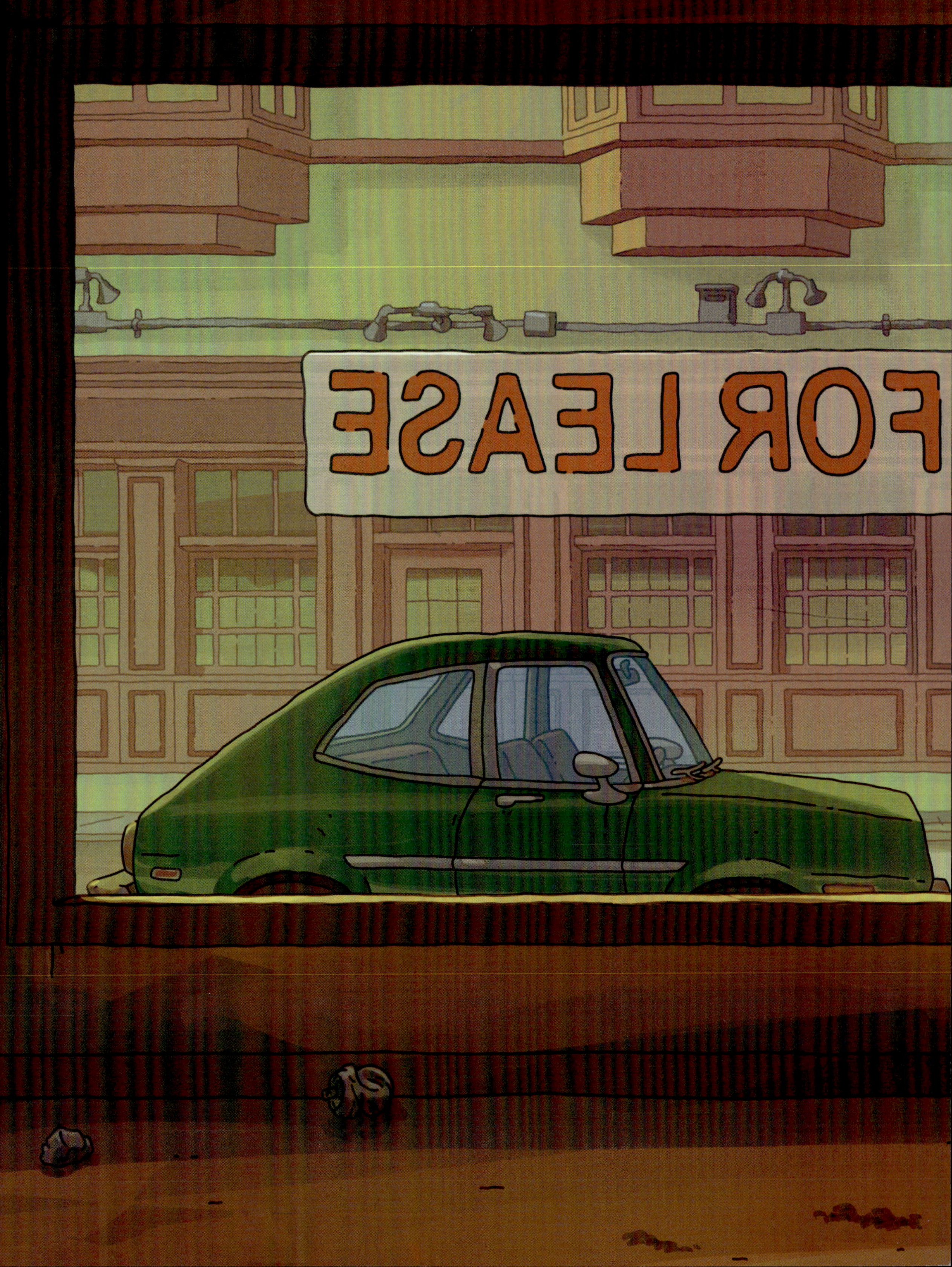

THE ART OF BOB'S BURGERS

LOREN BOUCHARD & BERNARD DERRIMAN

RIZZOLI UNIVERSE

TABLE OF CONTENTS

Introduction

When you're trying to bring an animated TV show to life, you have to "cast" your art team just as carefully as you have to cast your voice actors. In the case of the art of *Bob's Burgers*, there was no role for me as an artist—my drawing skills pale in comparison with the talent that's out there—but I felt ready to be a curator. So, from our little shop in San Francisco, we went in search of a character artist and a background artist to help us define the look of the show, and in both cases we found them right under our noses. Jay Howell was a rising star in the skate and underground graphics scenes in the Mission, but he was paying his rent working at Atlas Coffee, two doors down from my apartment. His mischievous drawings were laugh-out-loud funny and full of a randy energy that felt immediately perfect.

For backgrounds, all we had to do was look to see who had signed the murals near my house. Sirron Norris was also a Mission-based art star, and in addition to his signature blue bear, another subject he specialized in was the architecture of the Mission itself. He lovingly captured the tall, thin Victorian houses and apartment buildings that are rightly celebrated in San Francisco. Some of his murals of Victorian buildings are painted on Victorian buildings.

We had already cast John Roberts as Linda, doing that wonderfully specific voice, so we knew that the most natural setting for *Bob's* was the East Coast—probably somewhere between New Jersey and Long Island. But the good news was that there are Victorian buildings on the East Coast, too. What we especially took from San Francisco were the colors: on the East Coast, it seems like no one had the audacity to paint their Victorian-era building bright pink, or yellow or green, but in San Francisco, that's just a Tuesday.

Sirron was also heavily involved in figuring out how to animate Jay's drawings. He and Jay and an animation team in New York led by Dave Levy—along with our in-shop team of Nora Smith, Rustam "Rusty" Bekmuradov, and producer Ralph Guggenheim—brought the *Bob's* "presentation piece" into the world.

Fast-forward. We get picked up to series. We move our operation to Los Angeles. Casting the art roles has to happen again, and on a bigger scale. Both Jay and Sirron wanted to pursue the opportunities that were in front of them as hotshot freelancers, so Bento Box set me up to meet with a relatively inexperienced character artist out of Cal Arts named Dave Creek, and an experienced art director and background specialist from *King of the Hill* named Phil Hayes. Yet again, the first choices were the right choices. We hit it off with both men so quickly and appreciated their talents so completely that we met with no one else and offered them both jobs essentially on the spot.

Dave was from Oregon, and he was young and a bit wild, but his character drawings were brilliant and, in their own way, shockingly sophisticated. He was a perfect fit for us because he sought what was funny and quirky rather than what was attractive or sexy. He understood instinctively how big to make a nose, how round to make a belly, how to carry forward Jay's chinless, shoulderless characters into a series for Fox and how to populate the world as we added character after character.

As an art director, Phil was in sync from day one. He not only had a lovely line that wiggled ever so slightly, right where you would want it to, but he also had architecture in his veins. He flew to San Francisco and walked around the Mission and Noe Valley

taking pictures. Soon he had massive photo collages of storefronts and apartment buildings—enough to line Ocean Avenue and any other avenue we cared to create. What most charmed me about Phil, though, was his attention to detail in the interiors. He loves an outlet, that guy. He loves exposed conduit, and moulding, and bus tubs, and the little piece of paper that sticks up out of a cash register.

So we get our dream team, yet again. Dave and Phil plus terrific artists like Rosalina Tchouchev and Mike Guerena, who helped us define the look of the show and hit our deadlines and tell our stories. But we weren't done casting this crew.

Sometimes a board artist will emerge as a gifted character artist in their own right. Damon Wong is an example. I'd worked with him on *Home Movies* and I reached out to him as soon as we had a show. Even his rough drawings inspire me and others—they're that good. There was another board artist who joined *Bob's* in season one who would go on to effectively redefine the show, drawing by drawing, and that was Bernard Derriman. His rise from board artist to director to supervising director was faster than meteoric—he made that series of title leaps in just two seasons—but it was the most natural thing in the world. How did we find him? One of our season one directors, Jen Coyle (another superstar), spoke highly of him, and she wasn't wrong. Bernard's drawings became the lifeblood of our character animation and eventually influenced our character design, too. I'm not versed enough in the Looney Tunes story to know every detail, but I'm a child of the seventies so I know Bugs Bunny in my bones, and I think it's fair to say that Bernard was our Chuck Jones. He had a friendly, Disney-trained aesthetic, but his poses never seemed schmaltzy or cute; they were just funny and human, and he had all the other director skills, too: the right framing, the right angle, the right shot.

But there's more. Tony Gennaro came to us from *King of the Hill*, and he did that thing that people of great taste can do over time, which is he quietly but firmly helped us refine our look and our style. So did Hector Reynoso and Anthony Aguinaldo and Scott Moot, and Kat Kosmala, and Joe Healy, and Mikey Macasero and Simon Chong and Ben Chuang and the teams at Yeson in South Korea, and many more. Each hand that touched the characters or the backgrounds or the props or the colors or the merch left us better for it, and in possession of a show that now knew itself and could execute a dance sequence—or a lighting pass, or an ambitious background, or a T-shirt, or a promo. And that helped us move from a Sunday-night show fighting for a pickup to a long-running show that had earned its spot.

And it didn't stop with the show itself. As we aged, we took on a cookbook, and a comic-book series, and music videos, and merchandise. We saw fan art as a vital, inspiring part of what we were doing, and we saw even something as small as a sticker or a pin as an opportunity to grow our look. We saw each script cover and each promo poster or Comic-Con giveaway as a chance to sharpen our point of view. When we finally added Ruben Hickman to our team to help us as the production designer on the movie, we felt like a fully formed visual organism capable of rendering the world of *Bob's Burgers* in full shadow and cinematic light. We felt confident in telling stories set in a snowstorm, or a misty rain, or in a forest, or in that slanting light of early morning.

And now, an "art of" book! An enjoyable challenge: how to make a retrospective of a thing that isn't done yet. We're still making this show, still dreaming of ways to grow it. May the new chapters be as satisfying as the chapters you have in your hands.

—Loren Bouchard

EARLY DEVELOPMENT
Loren Bouchard: In the very beginning, we were thinking about a family with two kids—a boy and a girl. Here's Jay Howell's character line-up, and one of Sirron Norris's rough early exteriors. Why is Linda's apron bloody? We also thought maybe the family would be cannibals...(!)

LOCKSMITH
OPEN
BOB'S BOYGAS
GRAND RE RE REOPENING
OPEN
BB
It's YOUR
FUNERAL
Home & Crematorium

PARIS
NEW YORK
BOYGA OF THE DAY
SEX OFFENDER
$5.95
HAWAII
I ♥ BURGERS
NO SMOKING

MEXICO

louise
linda
bob
daniel
hairnet

gene
hugo
ron
mort

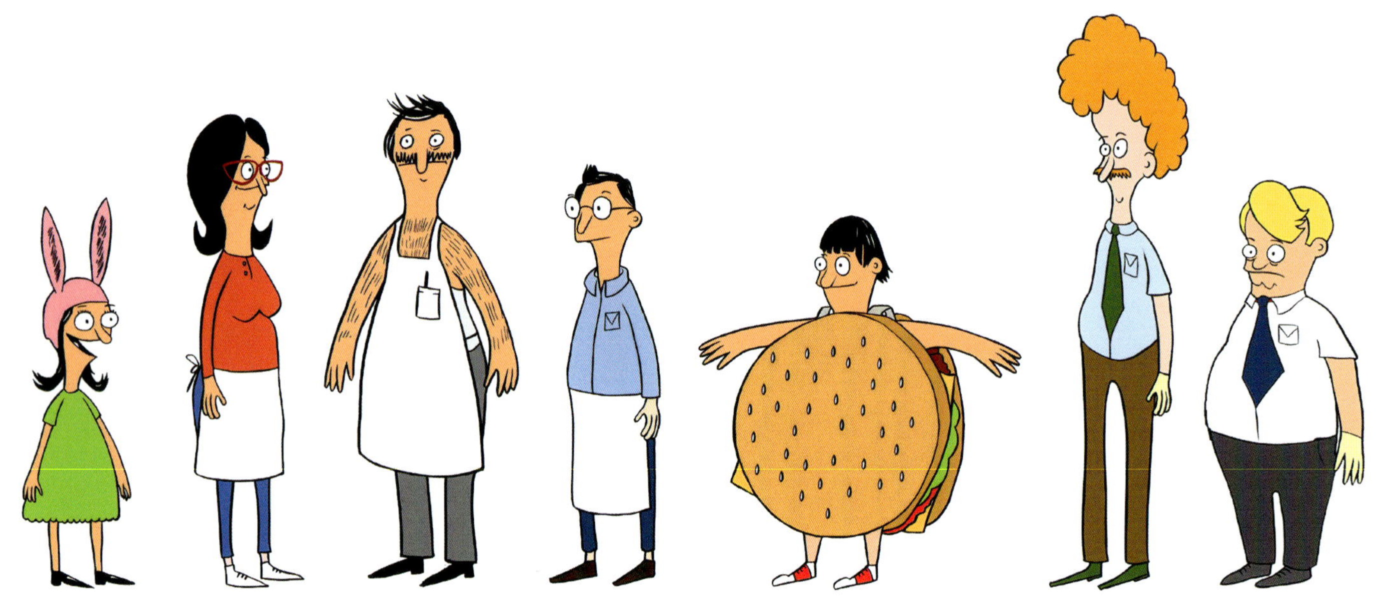

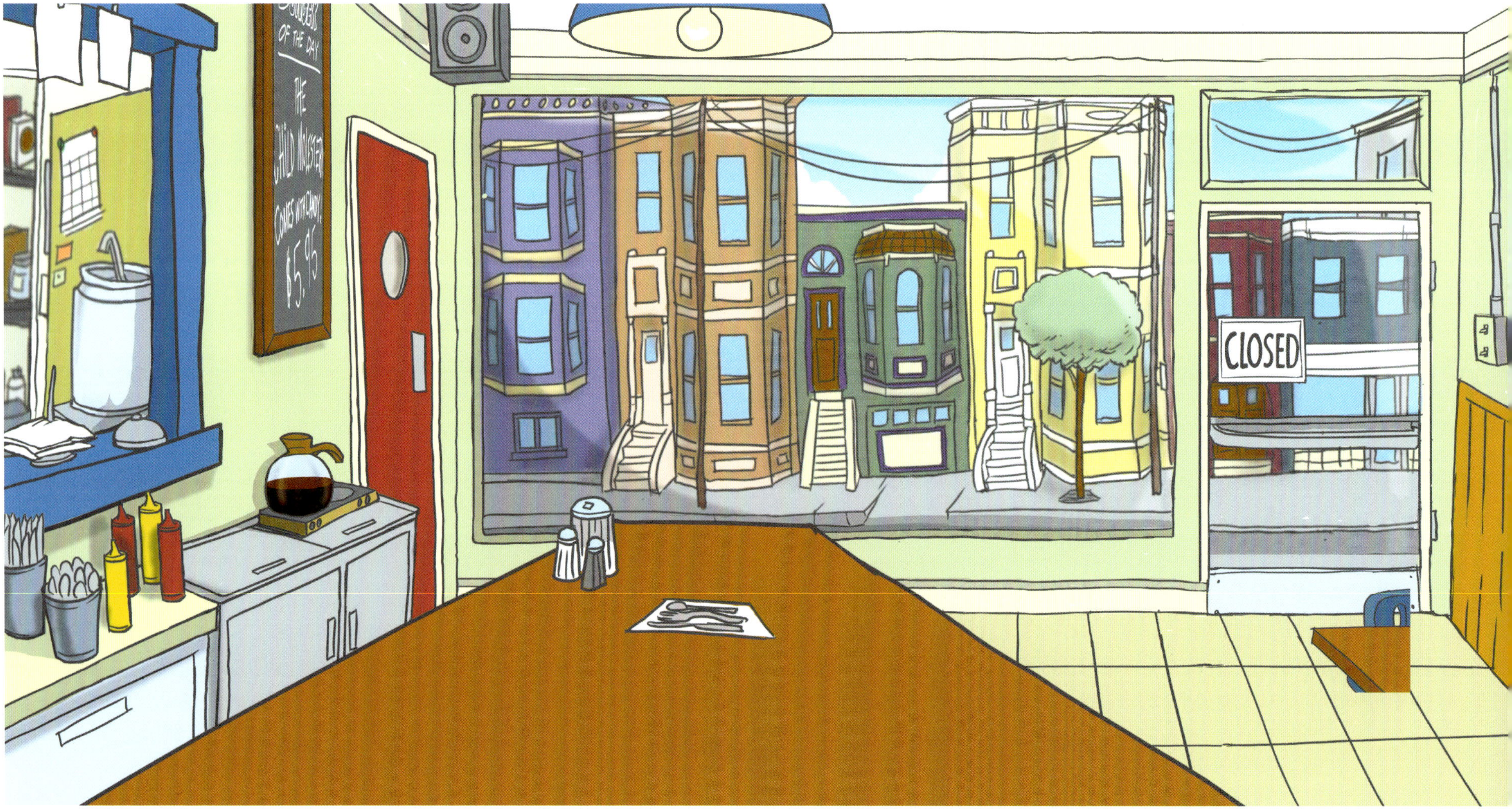
OF THE DAY
THE CHILD MOLESTER
COMES WITH CANDY!
$5.95
CLOSED

BOB'S BURGERS
BOB'S
BURGERS

KISS
THE
COOK
OIL

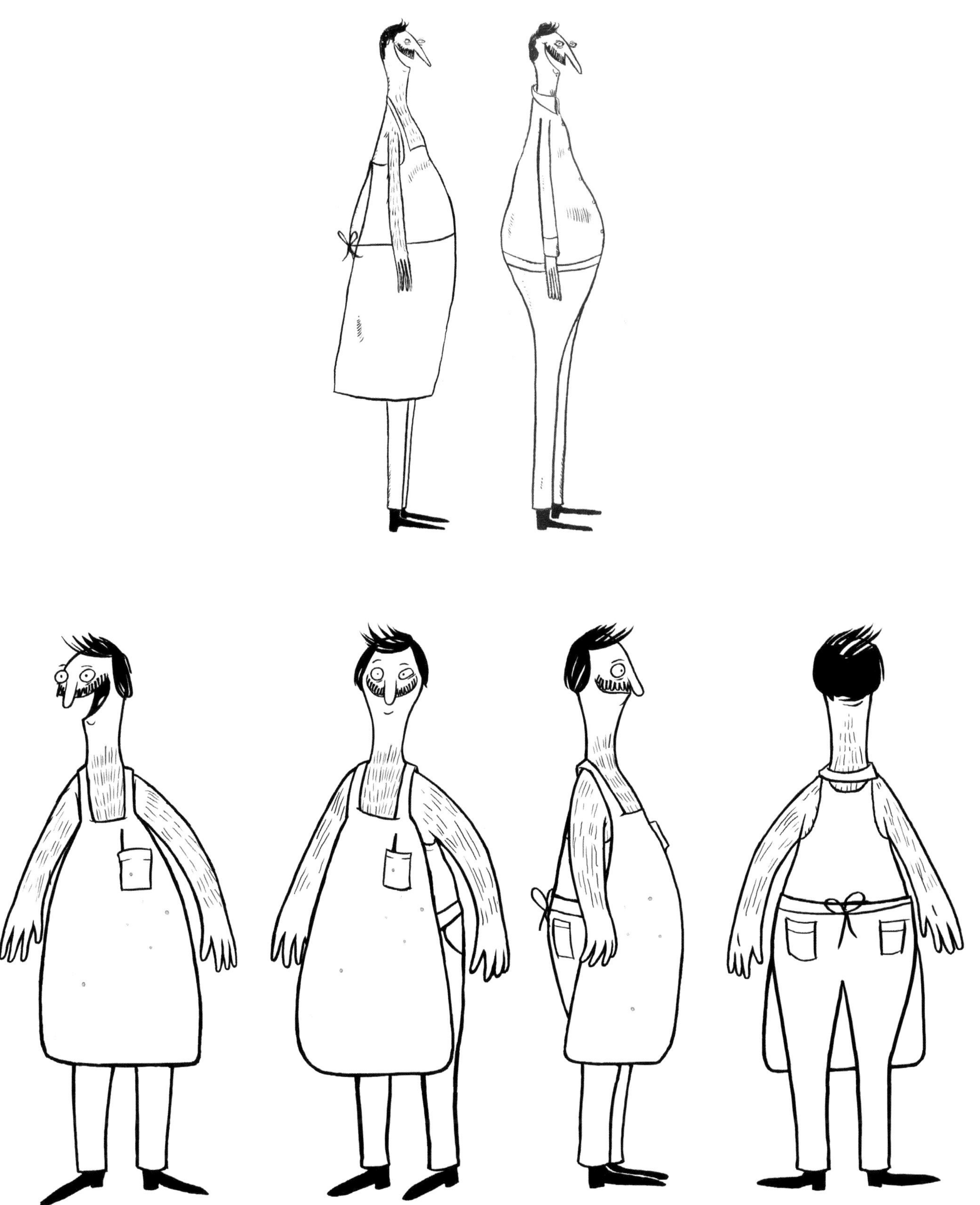

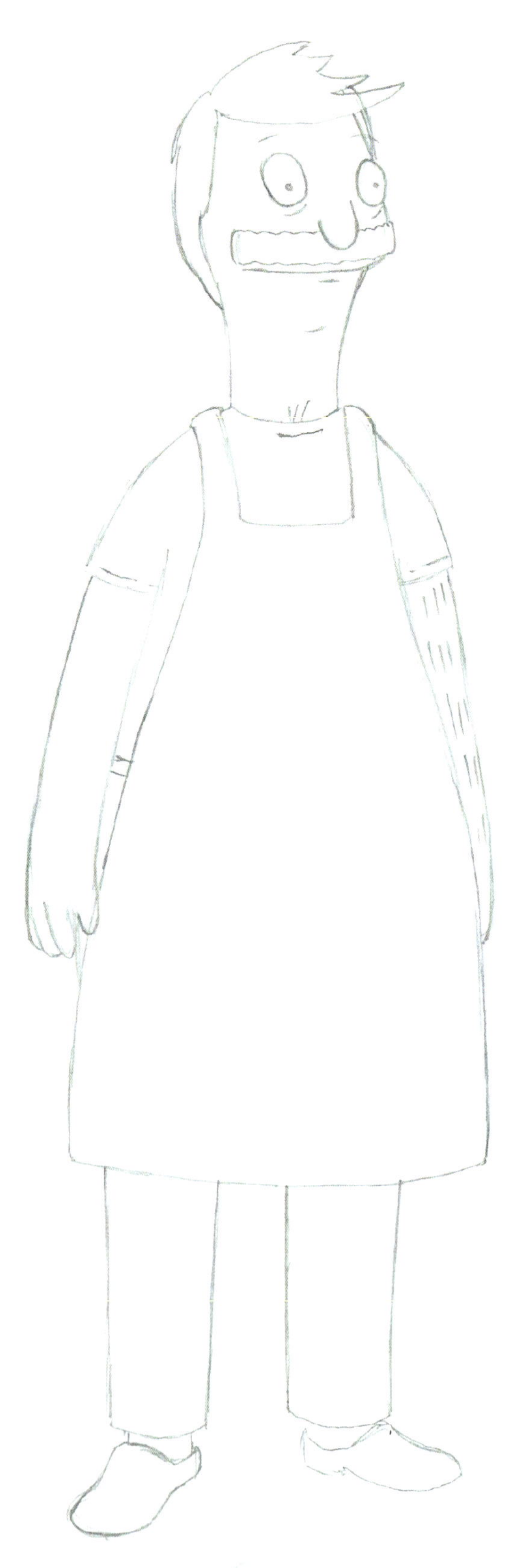

LB: I can't remember if the mustache was Jay Howell's idea, or Nora Smith's, or mine, but once it was on there, that was it. That was Bob. A mustache wearing an apron.

5 O'CLOCK SHADOW?
BOB'S GREAT GRANDFATER?
OLD PICTURE UP IN BOB'S BURGERS?
ALSO PICTURED OF OTHER BAD ASS MUSTACHE'S

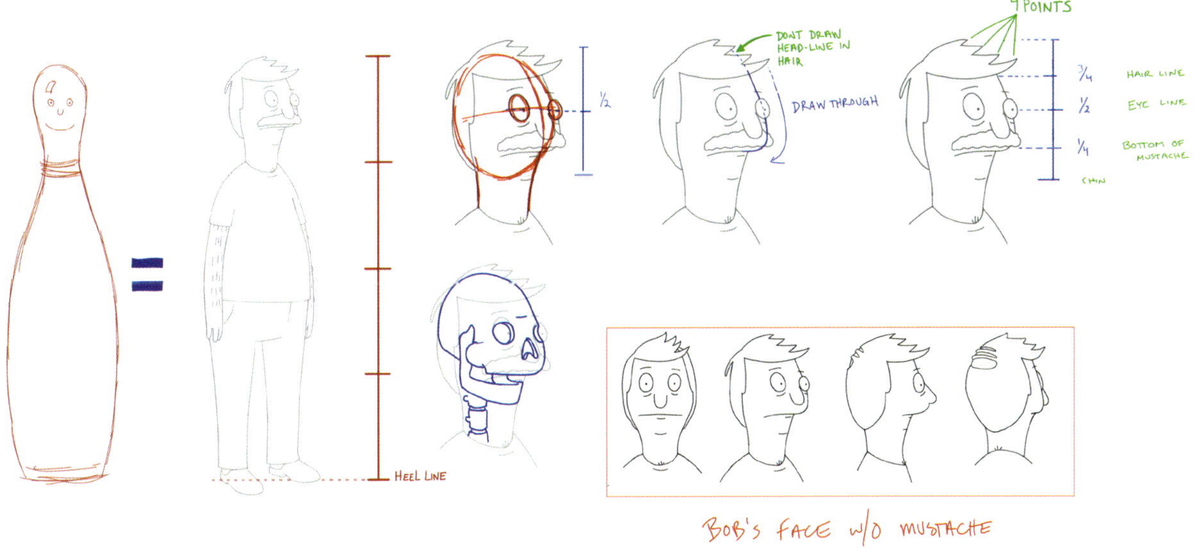
HEEL LINE
½
DONT DRAW HEAD-LINE IN HAIR
DRAW THROUGH
4 POINTS
¾
HAIR LINE
½
EYE LINE
¼
BOTTOM OF MUSTACHE
CHIN
BOB'S FACE w/o MUSTACHE

WASH YOUR HANDS!

LB: Linda's glasses were also clearly an early idea that stuck. Jay's Lindas had such a strong spirit. We couldn't have started from a better place.

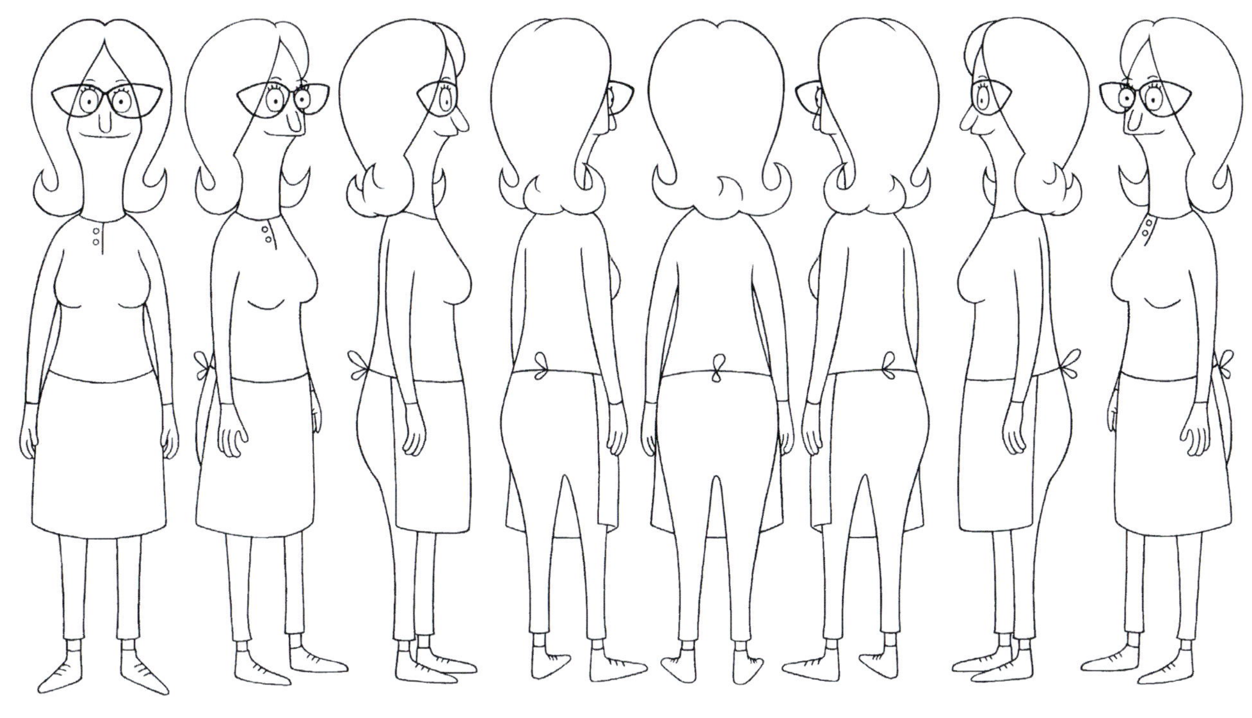

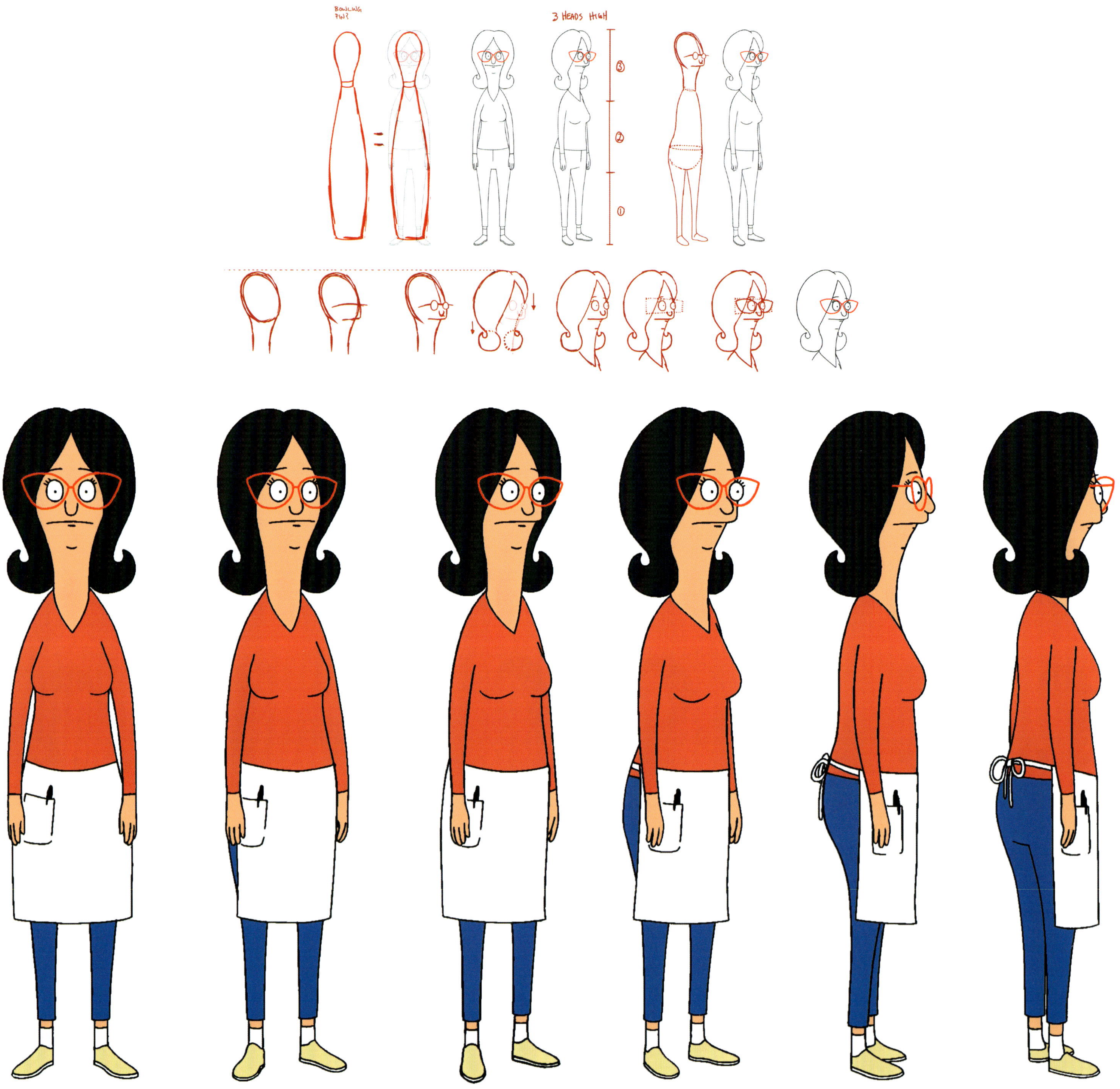
BOWLNG
PIN?
3 HEADS HIGH
3
2
1

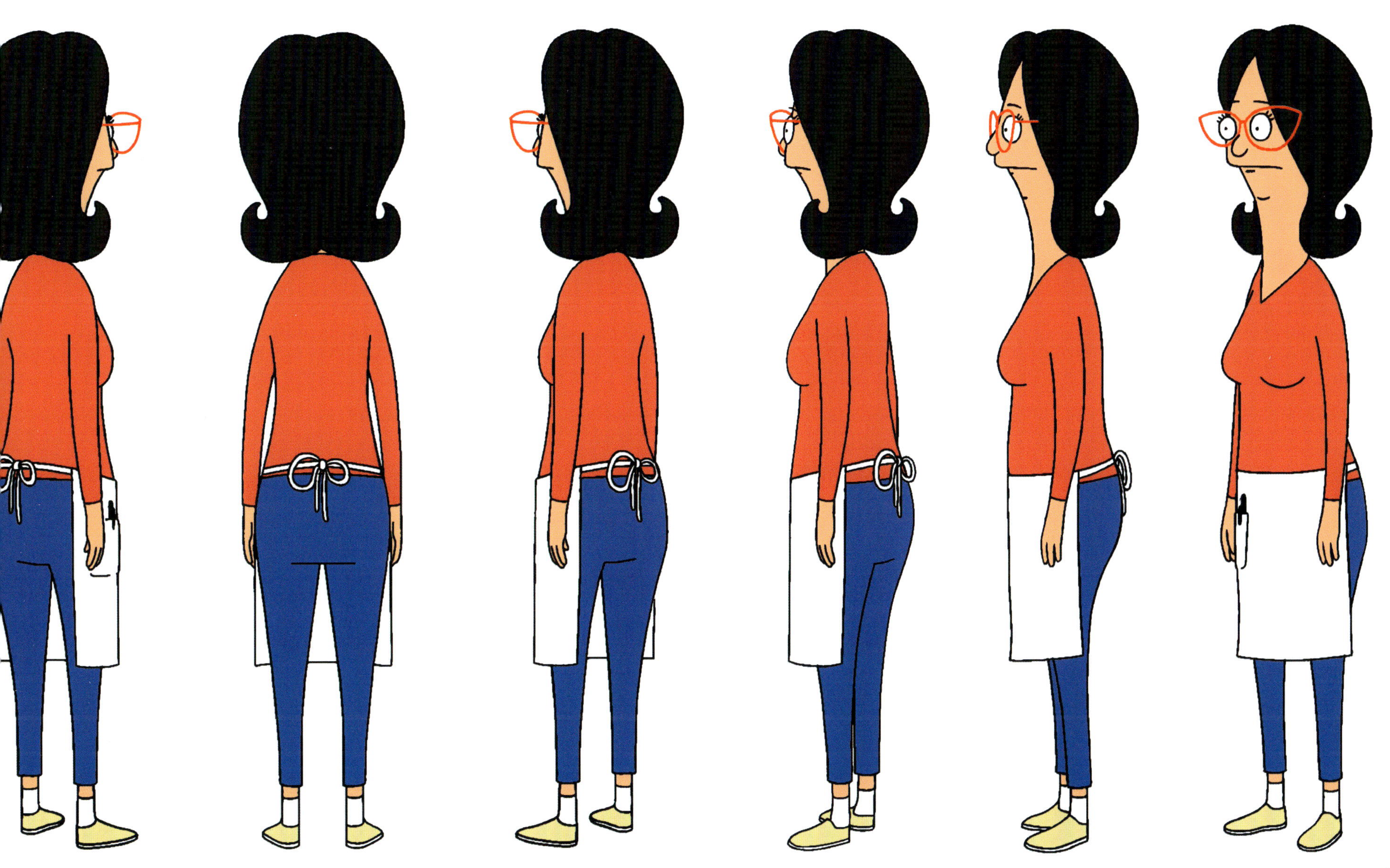

BARRET
THINNER CHIN
THINNER
HIGHER SKIRT
LONGER LEGS
HALO HAIR

LB: H. Jon Benjamin told me about this guy he had worked with who had a funny voice. We liked his voice, too, so we added Dan Mintz as a third kid—an older boy named Daniel. Daniel made it as far as our ten-minute presentation piece. The network thought the character was a little flat compared to the other people in the family. We proposed the idea of Tina and we proposed that she would still be played by Dan Mintz. This worked well for everyone!

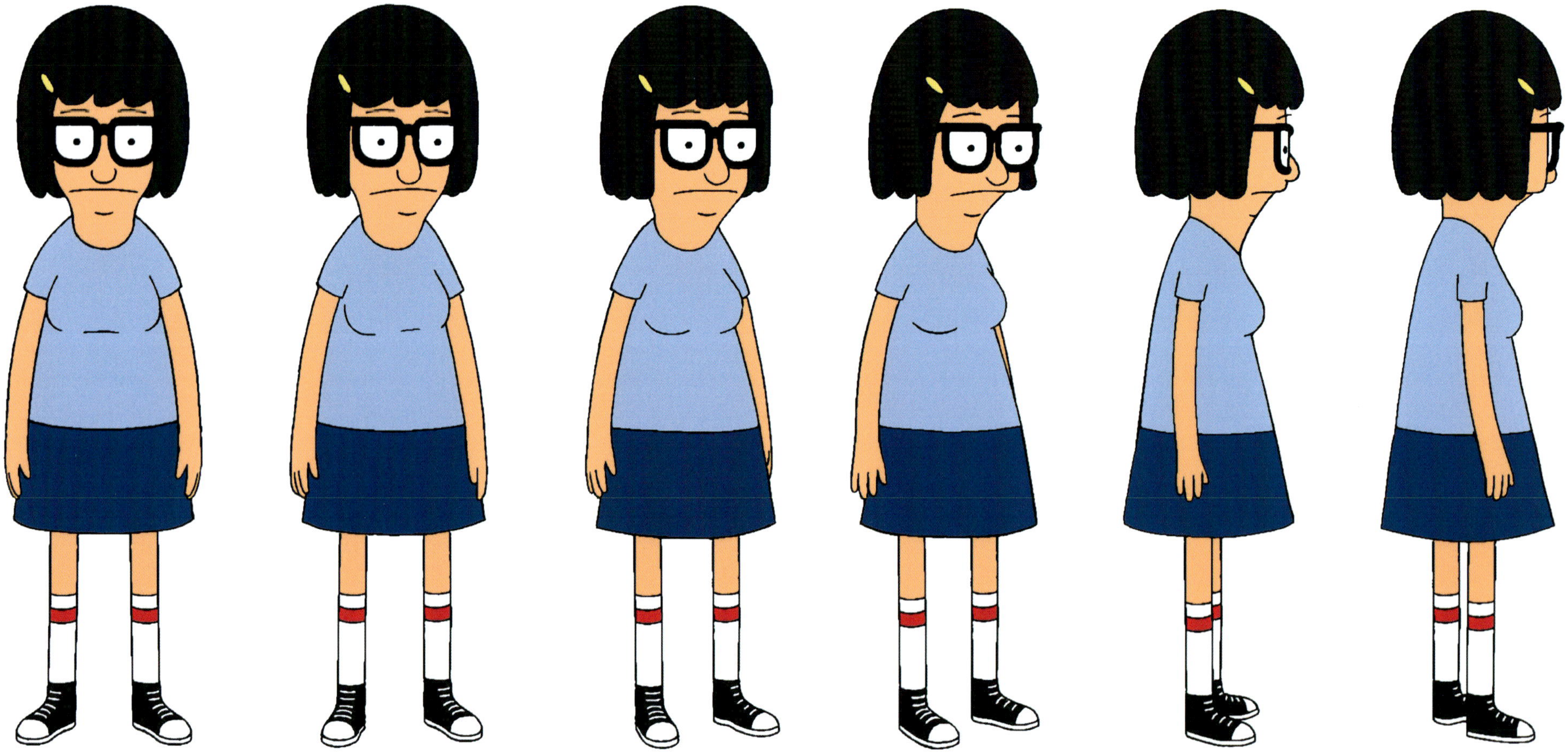

3HEADS HIGH

HELMET
HAIR CLIP IS RIGHT SIDE ONLY
THINK OF GLASSES
BEING A SOLID RECTANGLE
IN PERSPECTIVE
3 HUMPS
BANGS LINE
NOSE OVERLAPS GLASSES
3 HUMPS
HAIRLINE
GLASSES
NOSE
MOUTH
CHIN
WITHOUT GLASSES

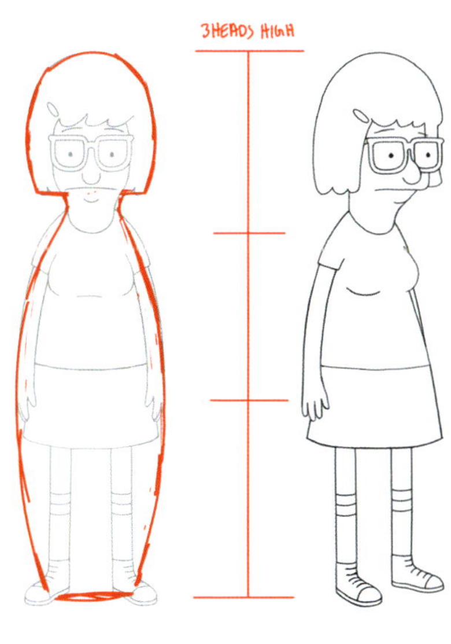

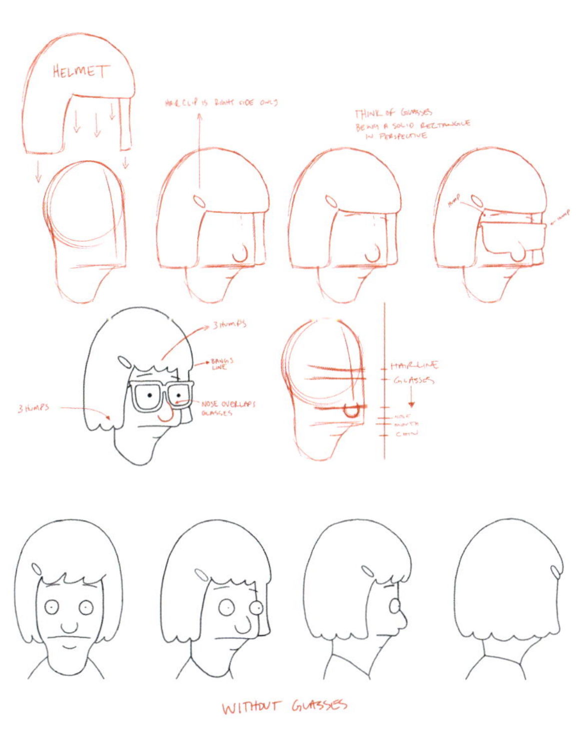

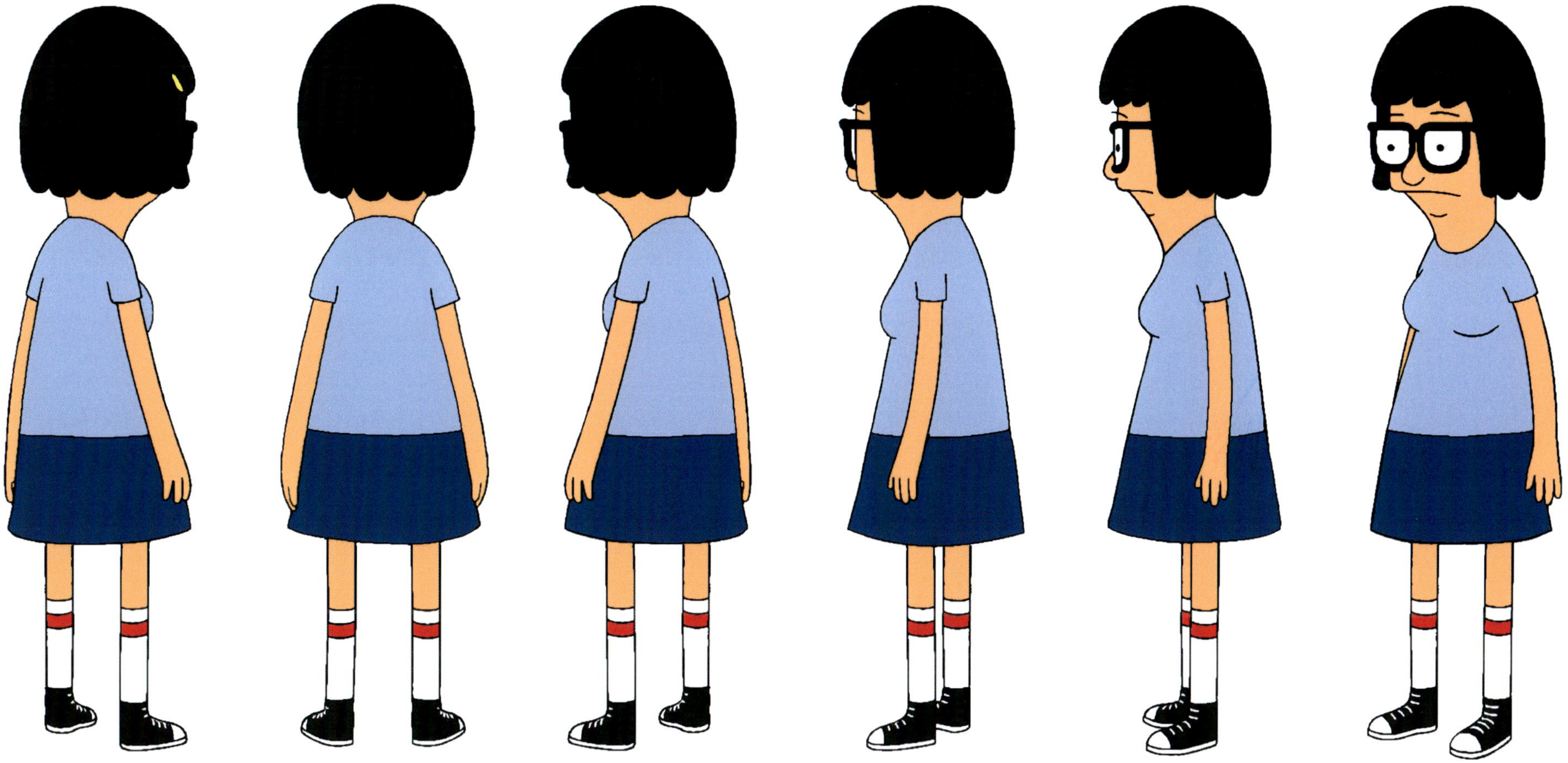

BOB'S BURGERS
BURGERS
OPEN

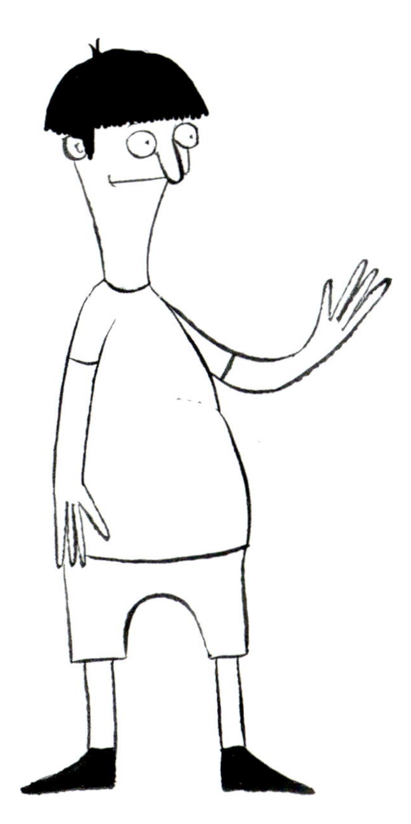

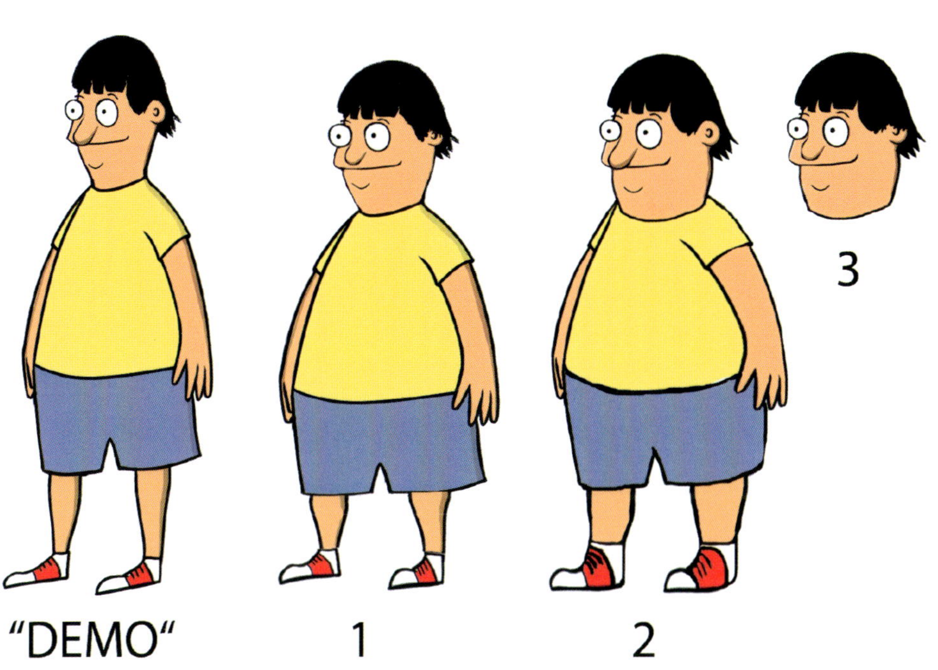
"DEMO"
1
2
3

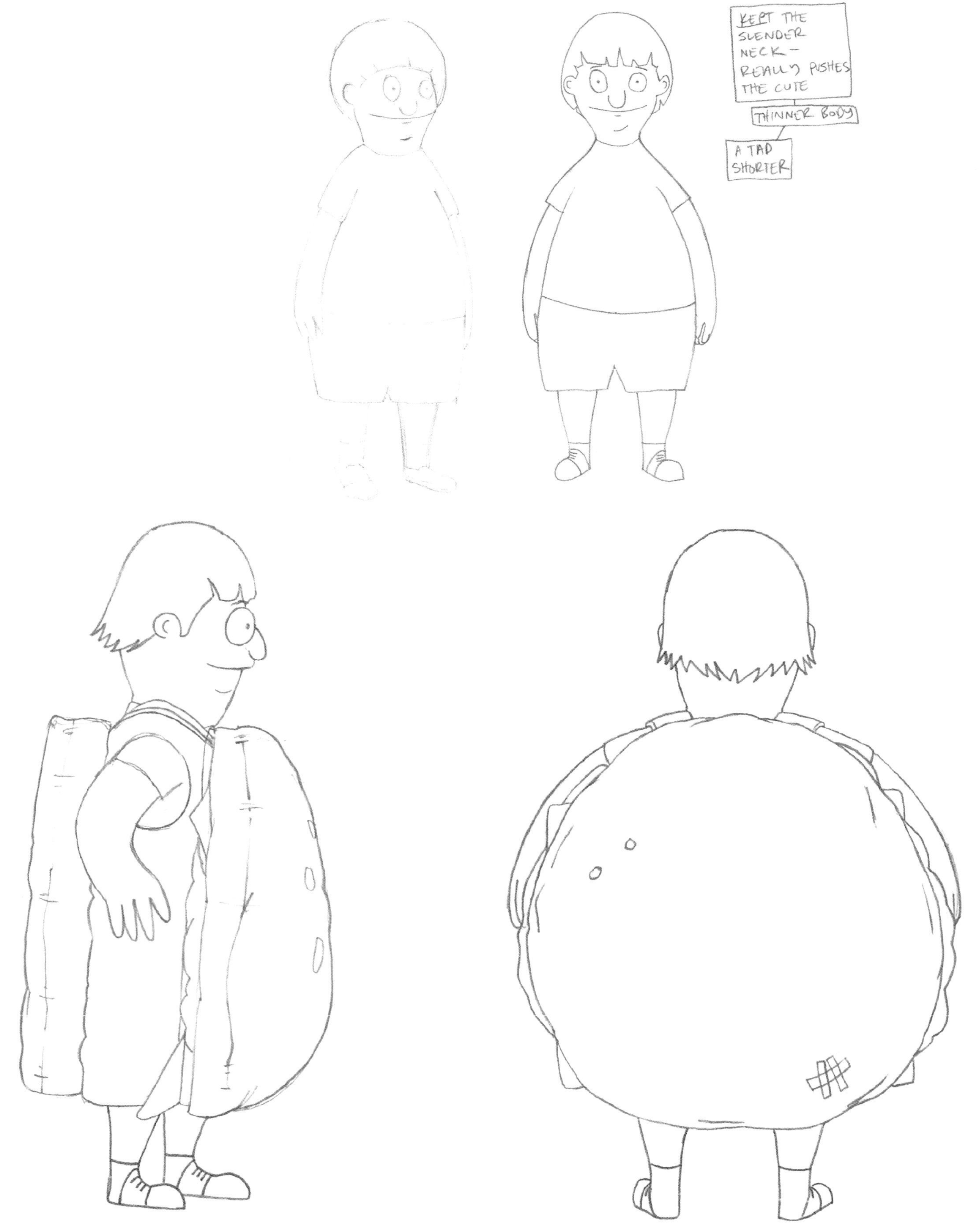
KEPT THE SLENDER NECK—REALLY PUSHES THE CUTE
THINNER BODY
A TAD SHORTER

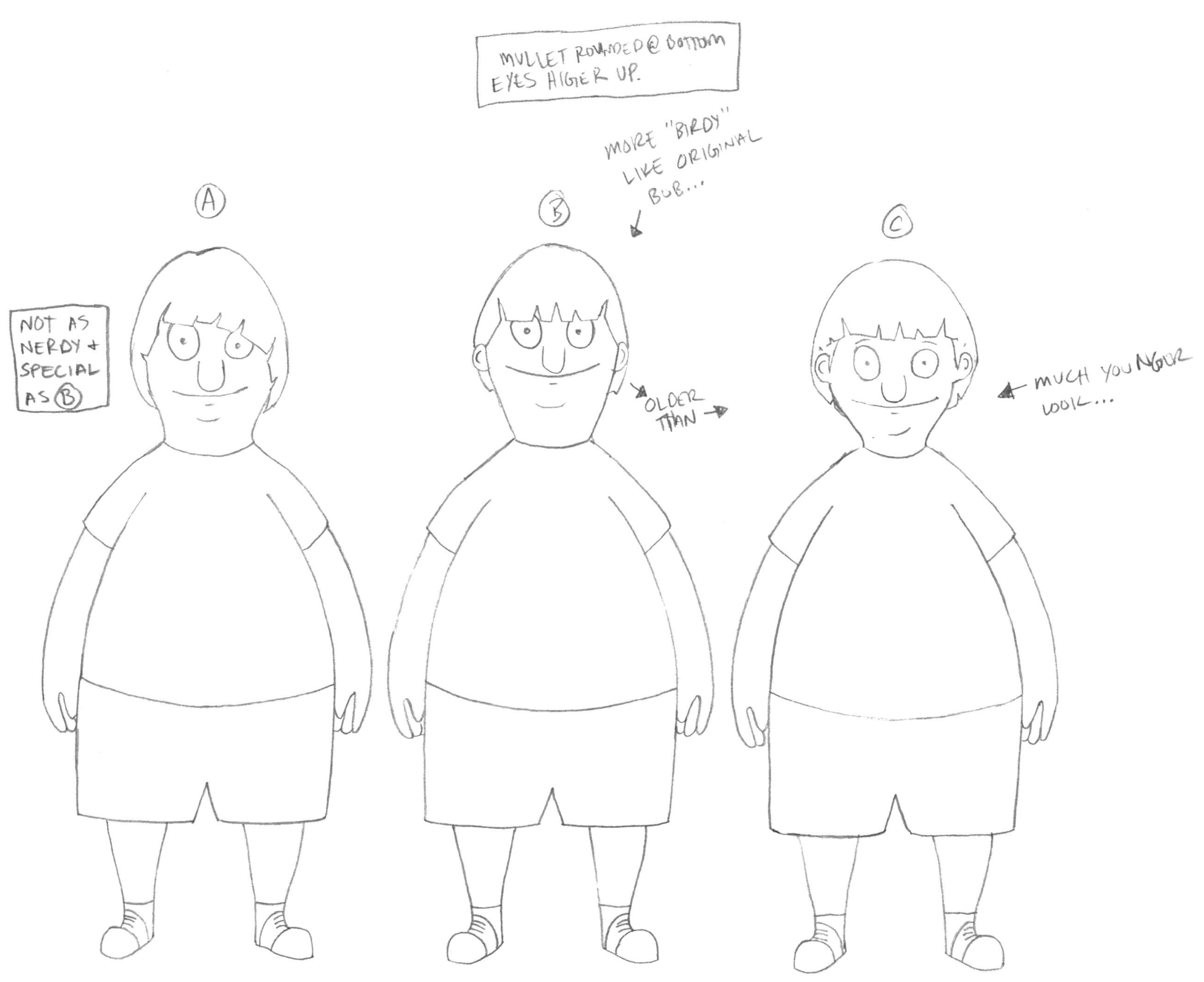

LB: You can really see the Muppet in Gene. I feel that the Muppets influenced all of our characters in a deep way, but it feels closer to the surface in Gene.

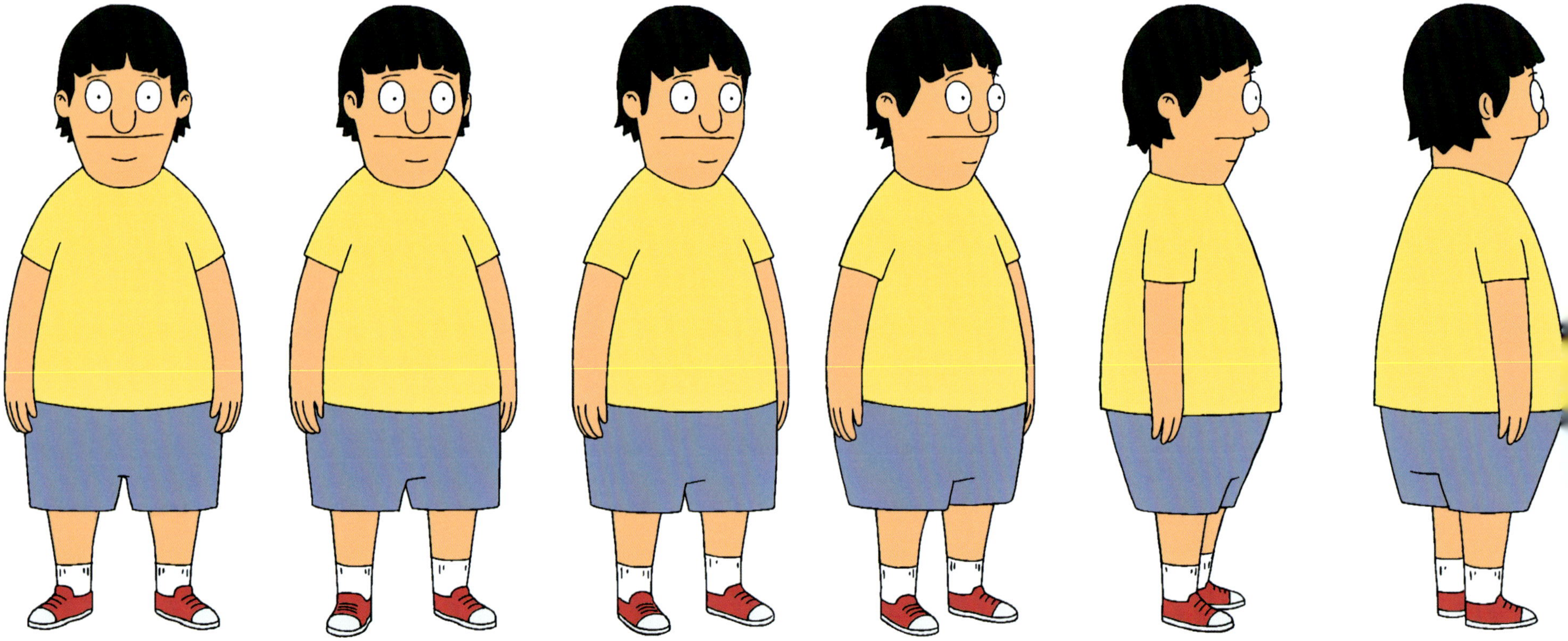

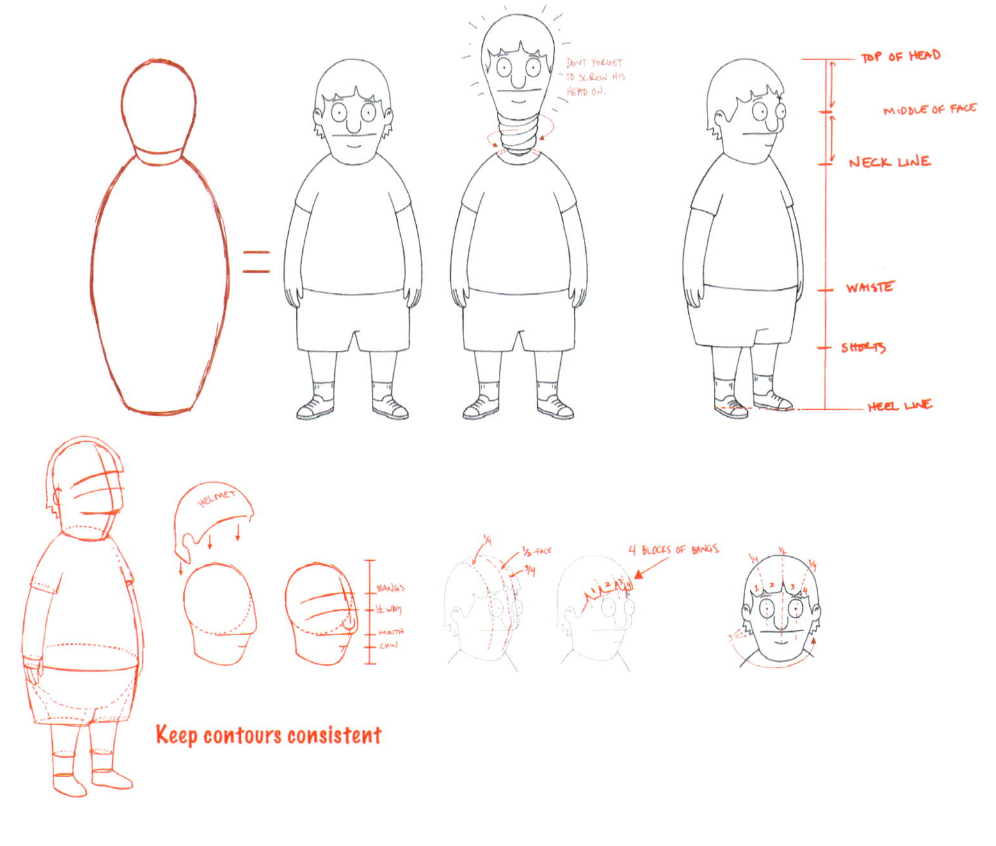

DON'T FORGET TO SCREW HIS HEAD ON.
TOP OF HEAD
MIDDLE OF FACE
NECK LINE
WAISTE
SHORTS
HEEL LINE

HELMET
BANGS
½ WAY
MOUTH
CHIN
¼
½ FACE
¾
4 BLOCKS OF BANGS.

Keep contours consistent

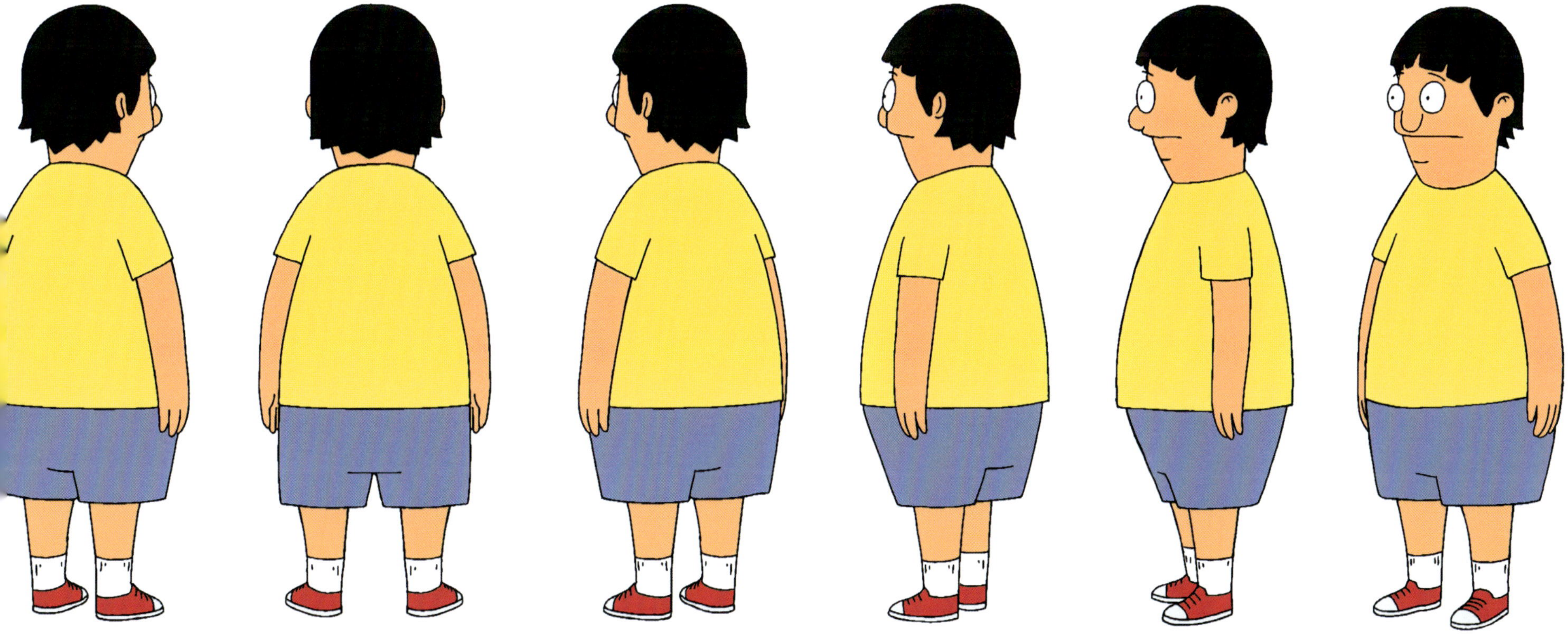

LB: The hat-with-ears idea came from a movie called *Tekkonkinkreet*. I was struck by the image of a small, young kid who always wears a hat with animal ears—how they can become an animal, in a way. There's power there. But of course, it becomes a vulnerability, too. Any jerk can break the spell just by snatching the hat off of your head.

GOOD SILHOUETTE
COLORS WONT CLASH
BUSY SILHOUETTE...?

EARS
FRONT OF STRAPS
EARS = CUTER
HIGHER PONY TAILS = CUTER
HAT FLAPS
FRONT STRAPS OR STRAPS IN FRONT OF TAILS...
EARS BEHIND STRAPS
NO - TOO FLAT.

SHE'S A BELL...
3 HEADS HIGH w/OUT BUNNY EARS
HEAD WITH BUNNY HAT IS ½ HER TOTAL HEIGHT
FACE IS MIDDLE OF HEAD.
COLLAR ⅓RD
FINGERS ⅓RD
UNDERLYING BODY
LEGS SAME WIDTH
OUTSIDE FOOT SHOWS ARCH
½
BOTTOM OF EYES
½ WAY LINE
3/4 LINE UP FACE LEADS TO EAR.
TWO
3

1ASA02_CH_Teddy_L_V01

LB: We added "Talky Teddy the Handyman" in episode two and he would quickly become almost a member of the family. This drawing (*above*) was in our archives labeled "Teddy." I don't remember it at all. It must have been Dave Creek's pass before we played him Larry Murphy's voice. Once we got him dialed in, he came together very quickly. I think the design perfectly matches the voice.

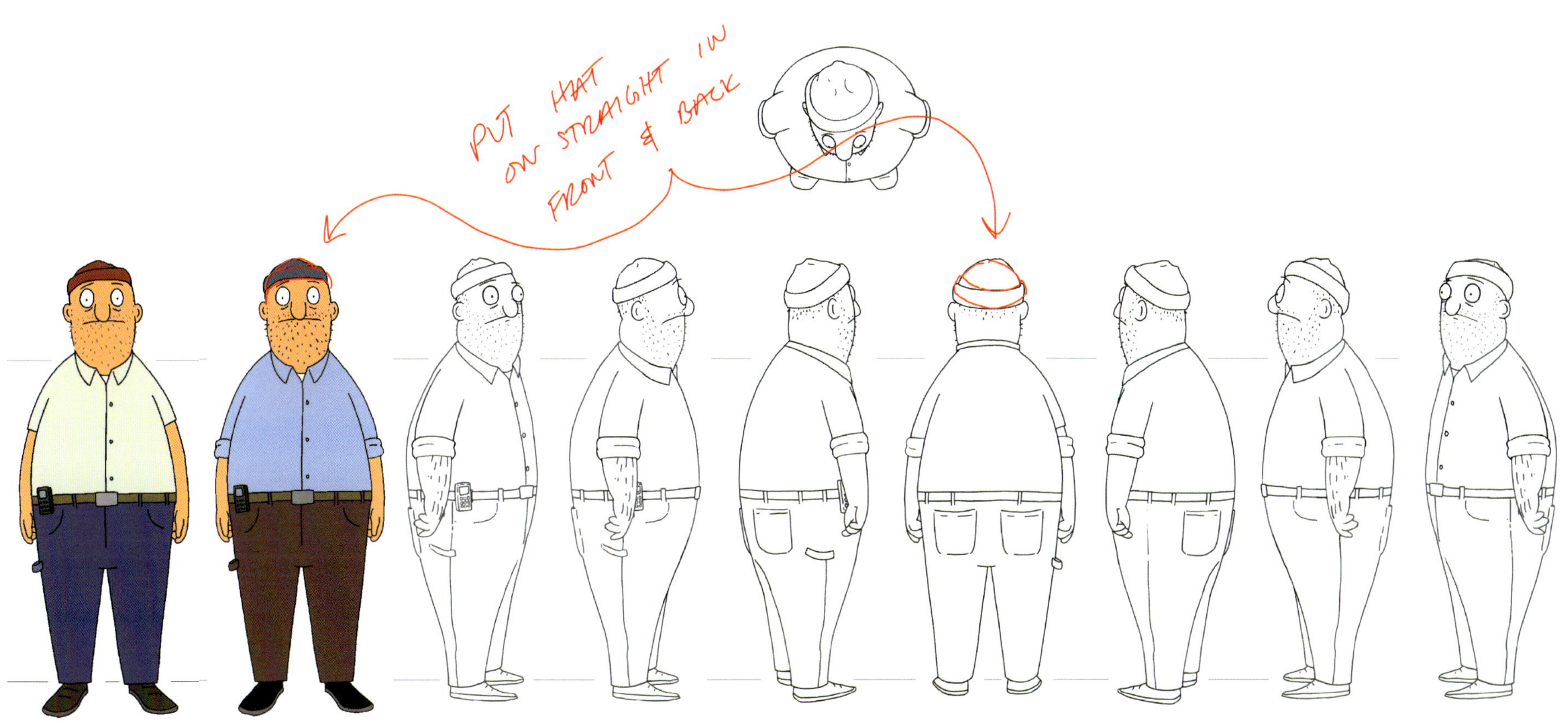
PUT HAT ON STRAIGHT IN FRONT & BACK

TINT?

LB: Mort the mortician. A kind man, always smiling and quick with a joke, and yet, he reminds us of mortality and death whenever we see him. And he's right next door.

BALD?
UNLIT CIG ALL THE TIME...

It's your
FUNERAL
Home & Crematorium

BURGER OF THE DAY
LET'S MAKE A DILL BURGER
-COMES w/ DILL
CASH ONLY

BURGER OF THE DAY
TEDDY'S SEAT IS THE 3RD DOWN THE COUNTER BURGER
5
2
1

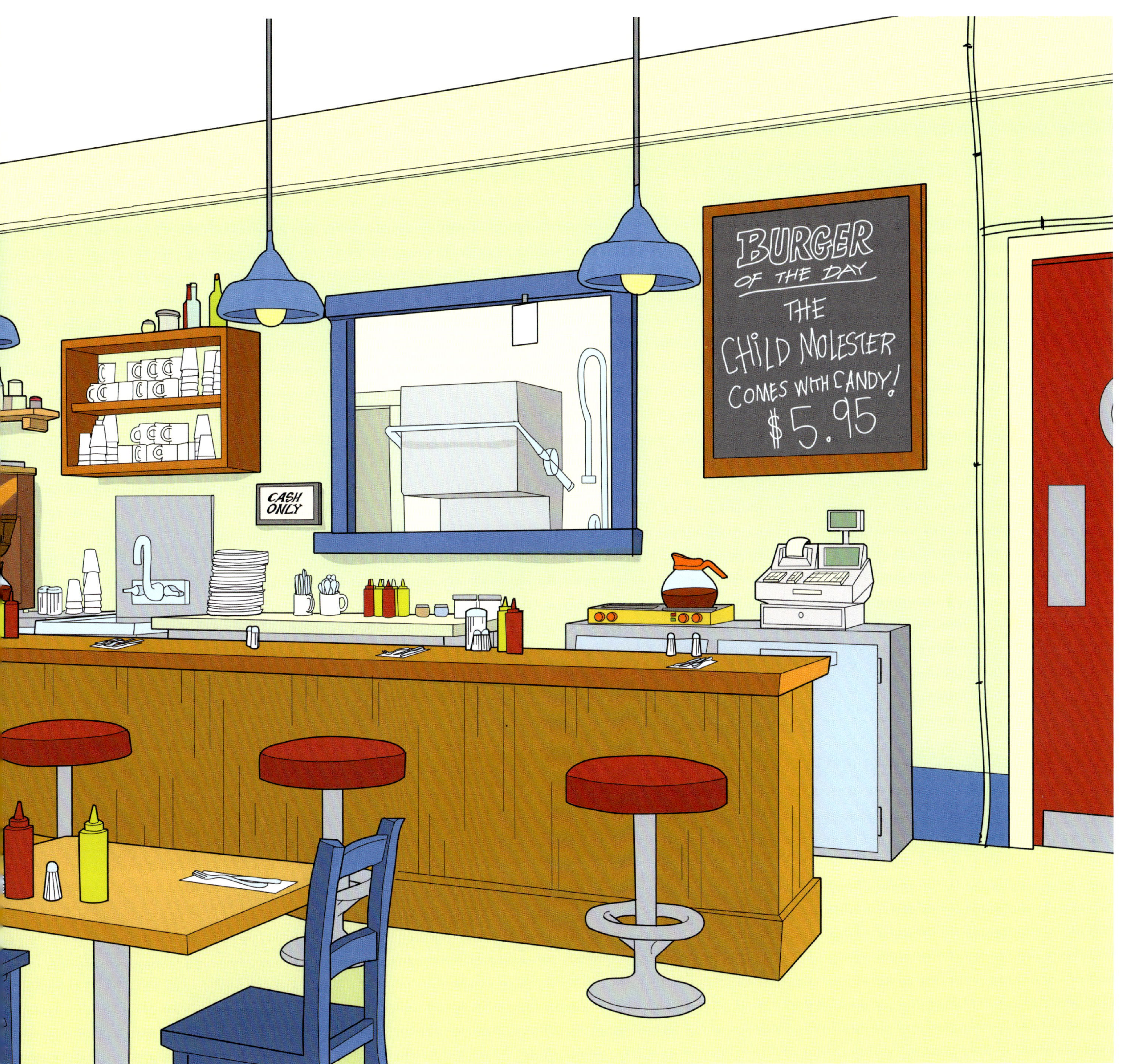
BURGER
OF THE DAY
THE
CHILD MOLESTER
COMES WITH CANDY!
$5.95
CASH ONLY

SC: 4 BG: PANEL: __/__

SC: 5 BG: PANEL: __/__

SC: 6 BG: PANEL: __/__

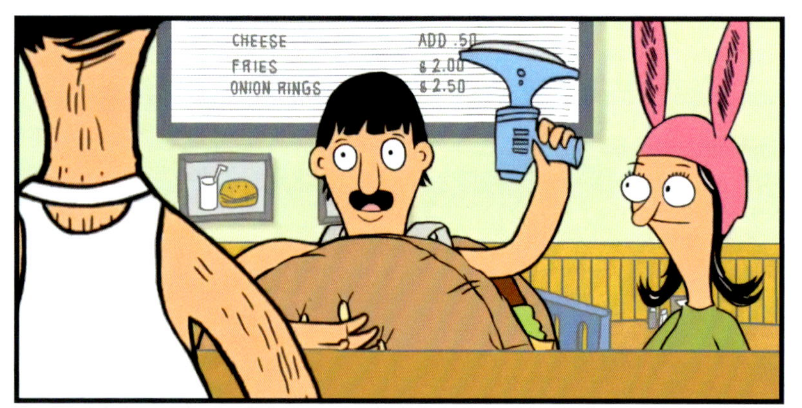

SC: 7 BG: PANEL: __/__

SC: 8 BG: PANEL: __/__

SC: 9 BG: PANEL: __/__

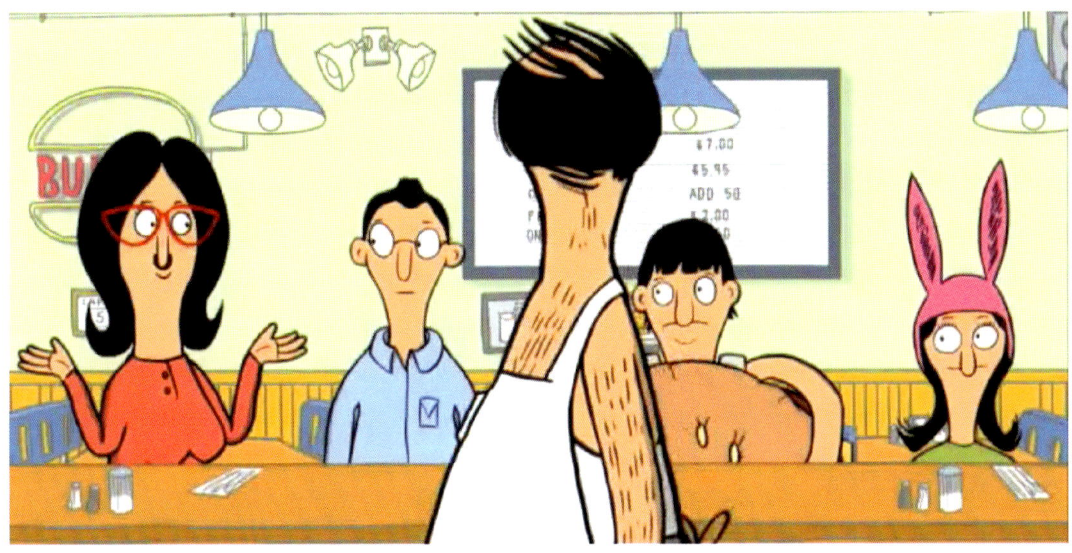

ABOVE:
Bernard Derriman: A shot comparison between the presentation pilot and final pilot.

OPPOSITE:
BD: A selection of panels from the presentation, back when Tina was Daniel.

BURGERS
REGULAR $5.00
SPECIAL $5.95
CHEESE ADD.50
FRIES $2.00
SIDE SALAD $2.50
SOFT DRINK $2.00
BEER $4.00

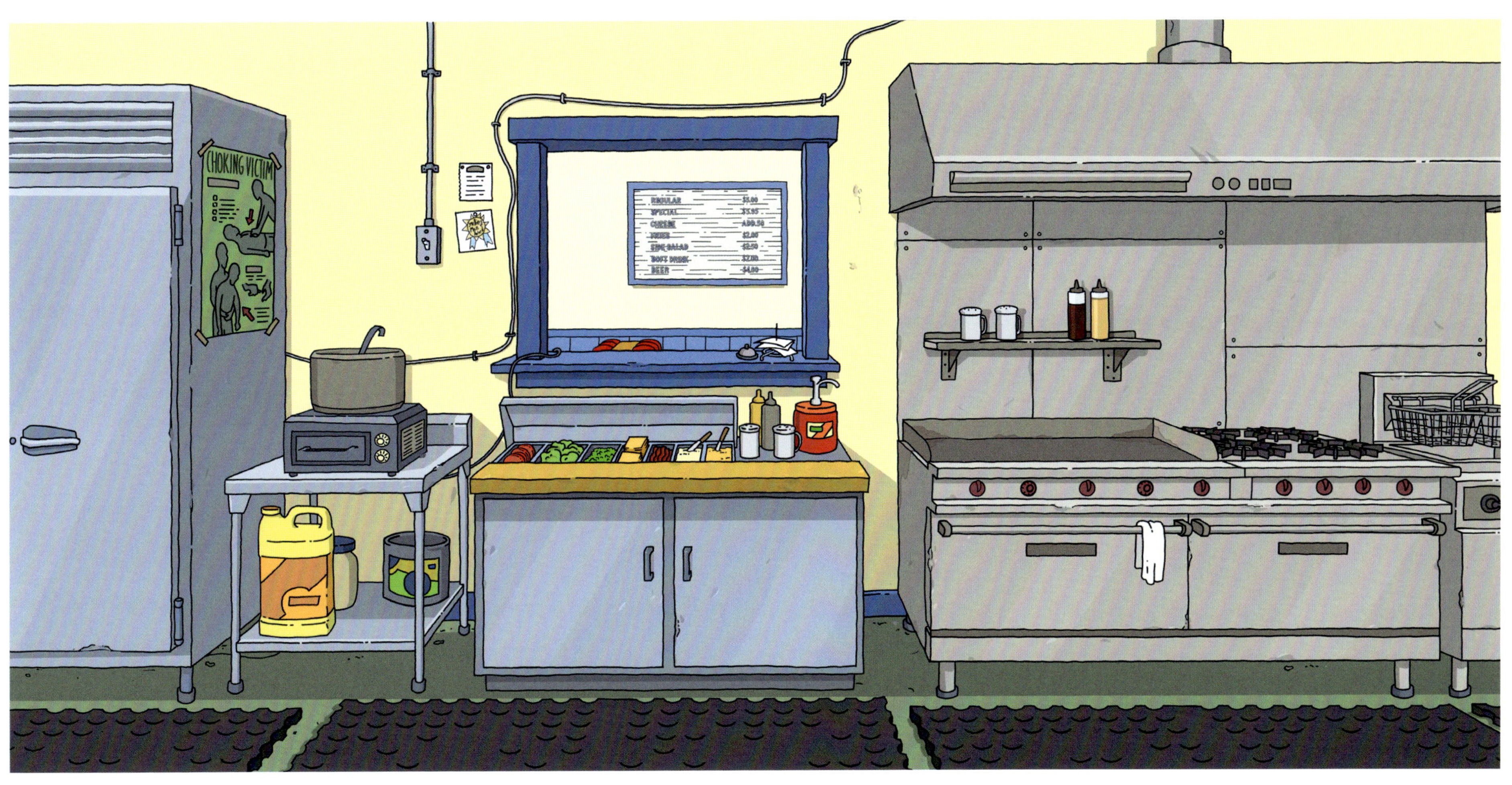
CHOKING VICTIM
REGULAR $5.00
SPECIAL $5.95
CHEESE ADD .50
SOFT DRINK $2.00
BEER $4.00

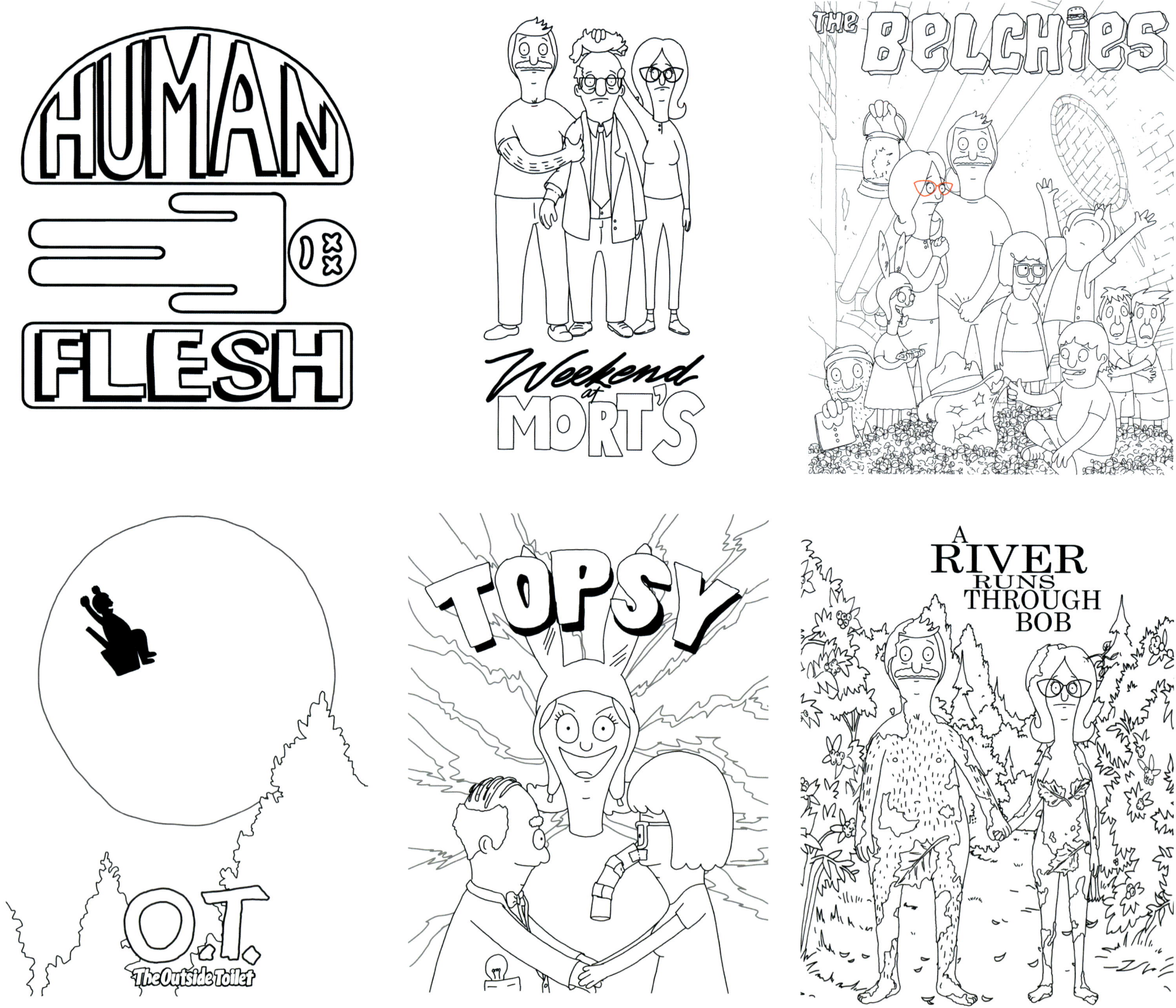

THE SERIES

LB: Every episode gets a "table read." We print scripts for everyone in the audience so they can follow along, and we make a unique cover for it. It's one of those extra effort things we do just for the fun of it. Tony Gennaro drew all of the covers until season nine, when he handed the job over to Simon Chong.

MUTINY ON THE WINDBREAK
BAD
TINA
AN INDECENT THANKSGIVING PROPOSAL
2ASA19
Friday, March 9, 2012
SEAPLANE!
Uncle Teddy
THE EQUESTRANAUTS

W
GENE IT ON

WHARF HORSE
OR HOW BOB SAVES/DESTROYS THE TOWN PART 1

WORLD WHARF II
THE WHARFENING
OR HOW BOB SAVES/DESTROYS THE TOWN PART 2

Friends With Burger-fits

MIDDAY
RUN

FATHER OF THE BOB
BIG BOB'S
DINER

Late Afternoon in the Garden of Bob & Louise

SPEAKEASY
RIDER
26

The
Millie-c
Candi

THE RUNWAY CLUB

The
Itty Bitty Ditty
Committee

A VIEW
TO A SPILL

BUS
EAT SPRAY LINDA

OEDE

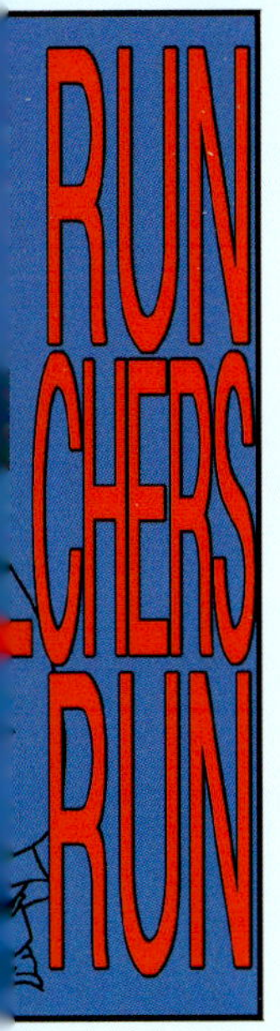
RUN
CHERS
RUN

TINA AND THE REAL GHOST

TINA TAILOR SOILDER SPY

Work Hard or
DIE TRYING, Girl

DAWN OF THE PECK

CAN'T BUY ME
MATH

The GAYLE TALES

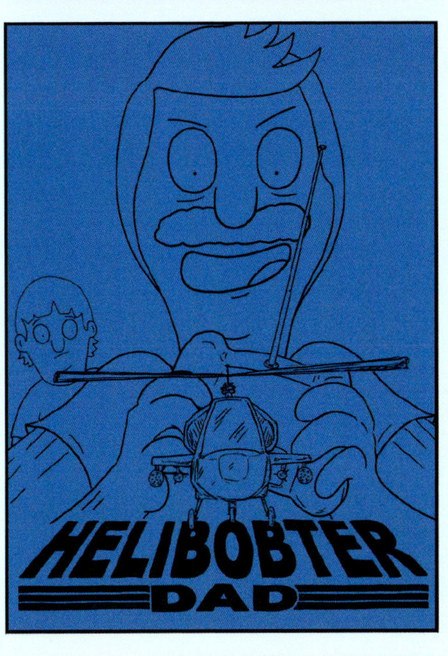
HELIBOBTER
DAD

ADVENTURES
CHINCHILLA SITTING

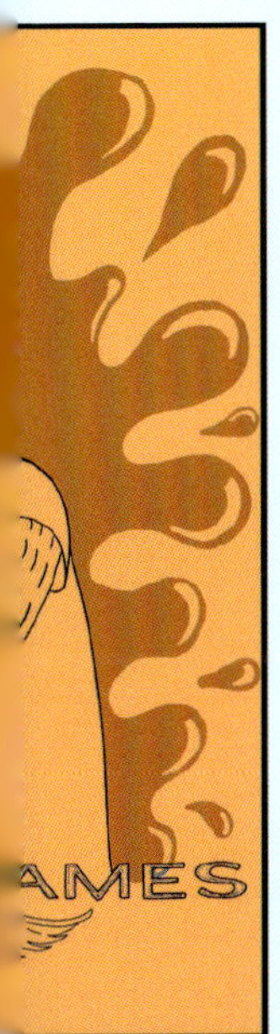
AMES

鷹と雛
Hawk & Chick

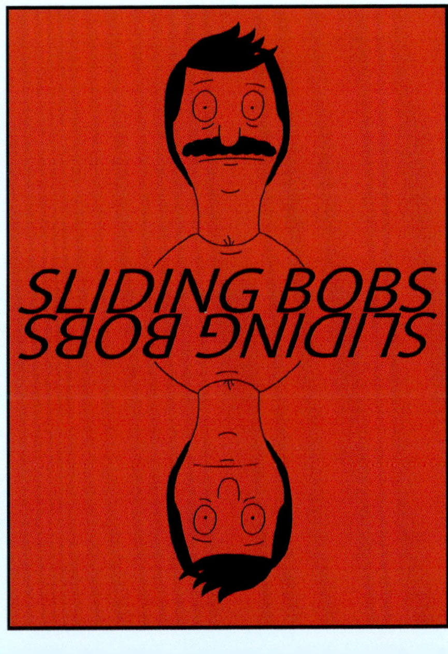
SLIDING BOBS
SLIDING BOBS

spray
anything

THE COOK, THE STEVE,
THE GAYLE, & HER LOVER

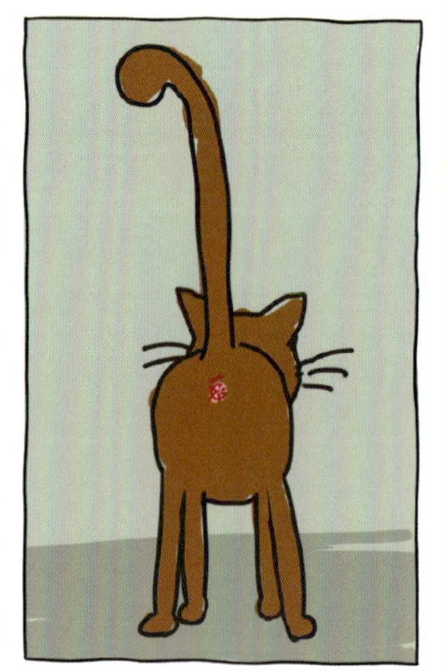

LB: Some episodes require some very special designs.

CAFFREY'S
Taffy
DANGER
KEEP OUT

NO TRESSPASSING

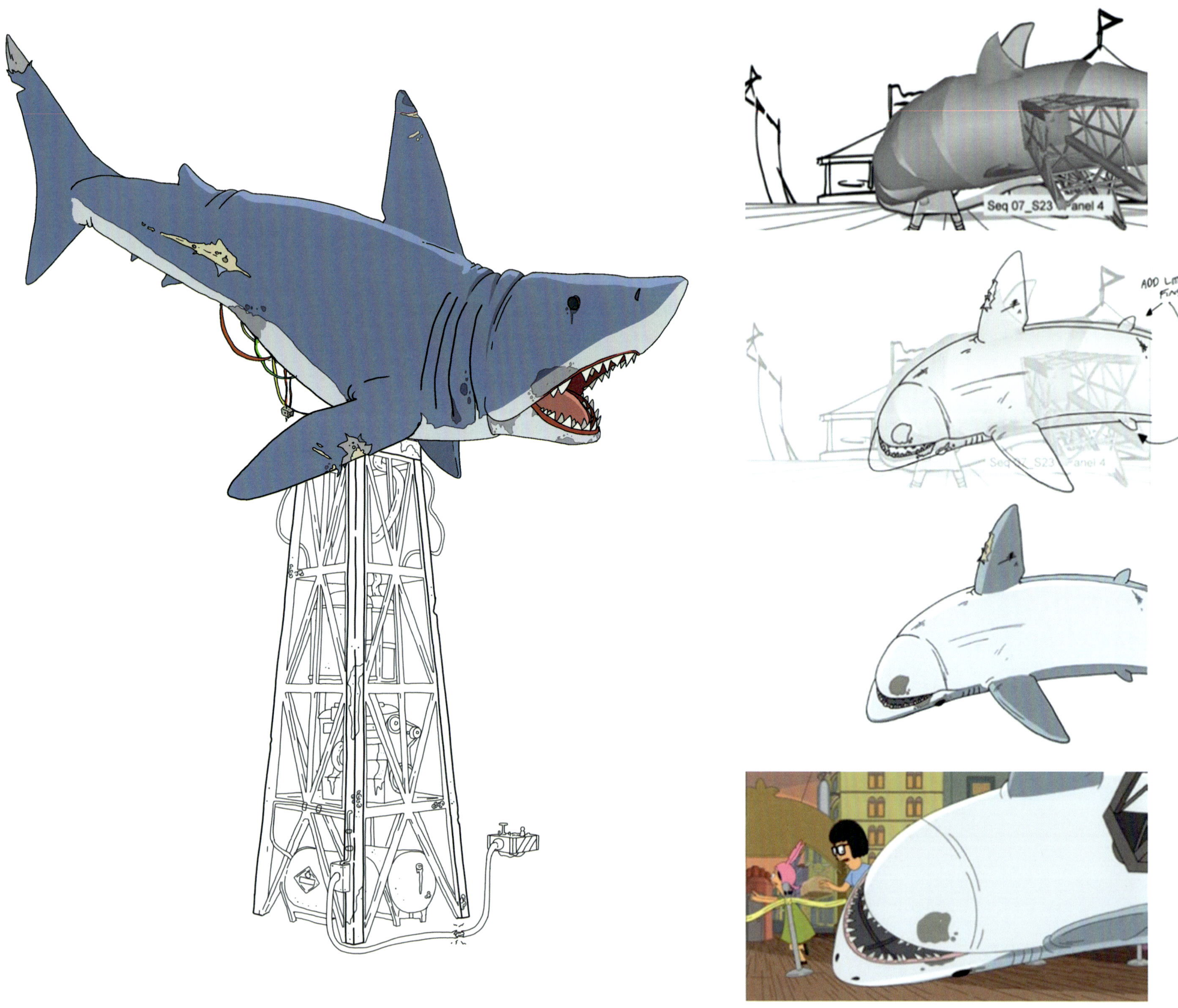

BD: Season two's "The Deepening" was the first episode to utilize 3D animation on *Bob's*. We built a mechanical shark in 3D using Maya. We drew over all of the 3D images to make sure that the animation wasn't too smooth and matched the look of the rest of the show. Only the major keys were sent to the overseas animation studio.

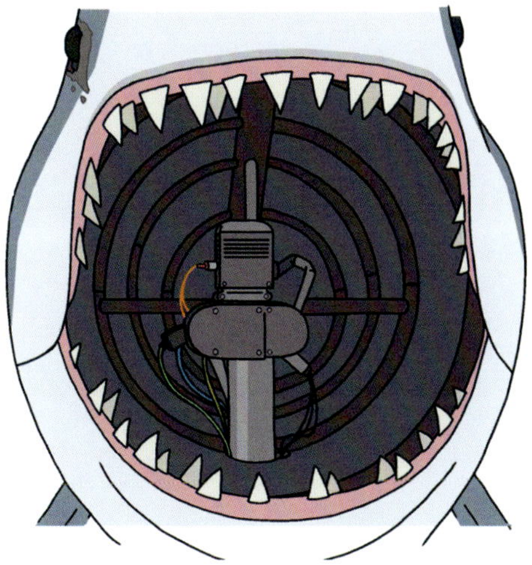

BD: Continuity is an interesting aspect of *Bob's Burgers*. In some ways nothing ever changes, but here and there we like to let events leave their marks on future episodes. In the climax of "The Deepening," the mechanical shark chews on the soft-serve ice cream machine in the restaurant. In every episode since, the teeth-marks are still visible on the side of the machine.

DINER
OPEN
PHONE

DINER

WONDER
WHARF
PRIZES
SKEE-BALL
GAMES
HOT DOGS

LB: We love backgrounds that blend beauty and grit. We love bright hits of color and evocative details that make a place feel real and specific. You can find this quality in background paintings of something as grand as a carousel on Wonder Wharf, or in details as small as an outlet on a wall.

ARCADE

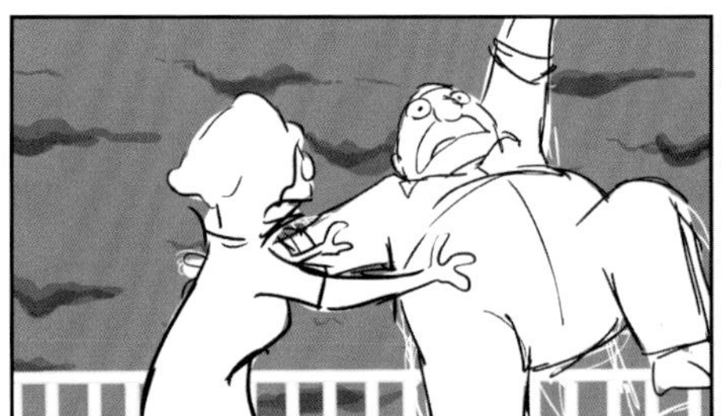

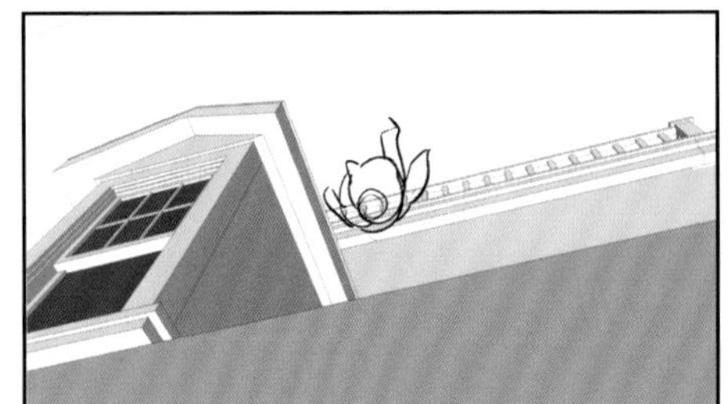
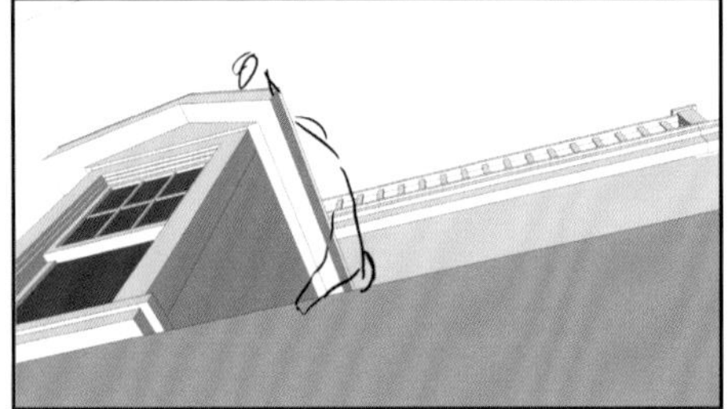
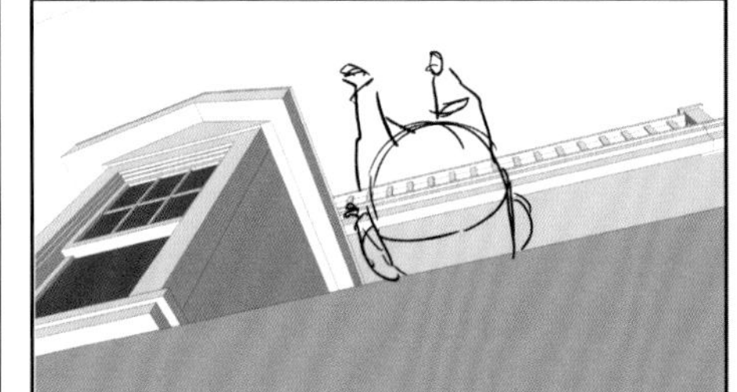
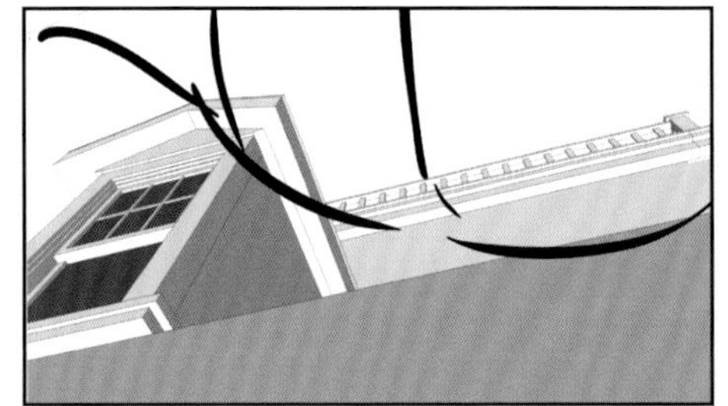

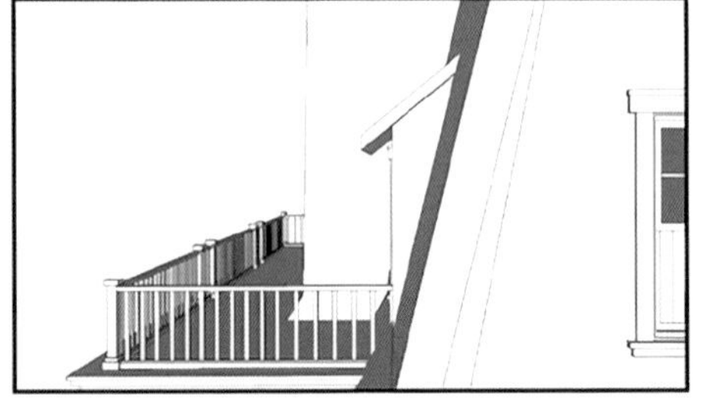
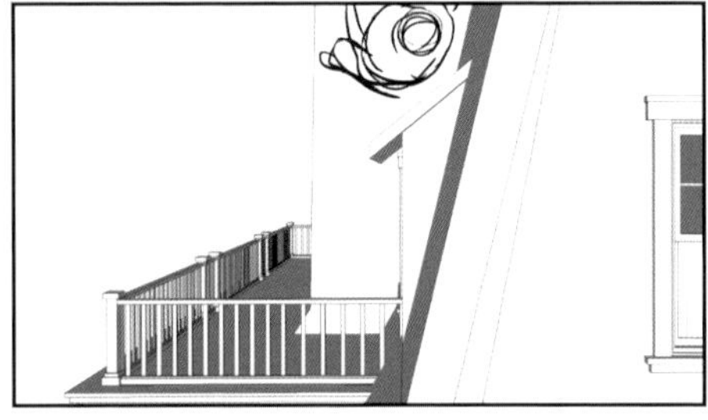
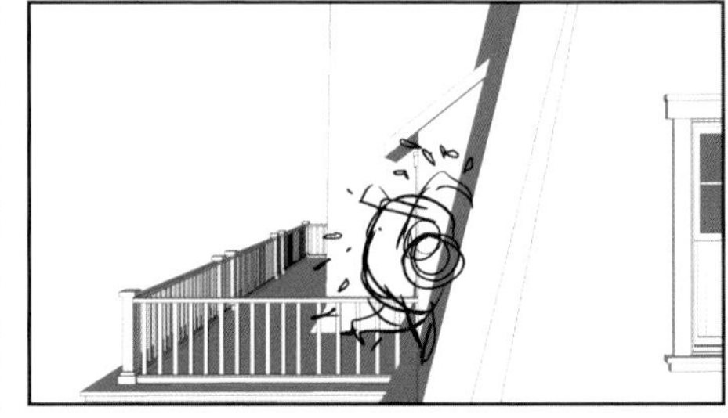

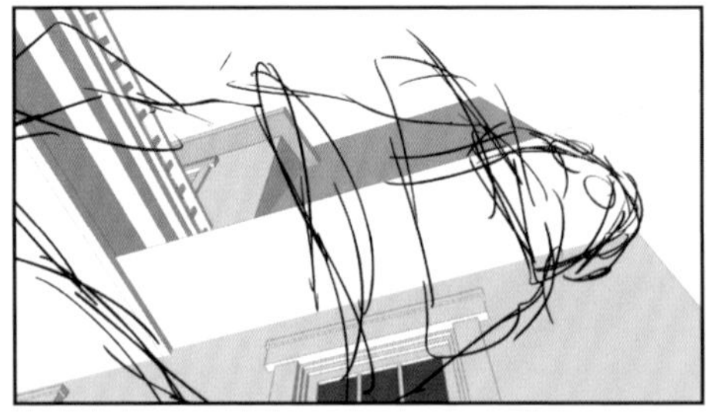

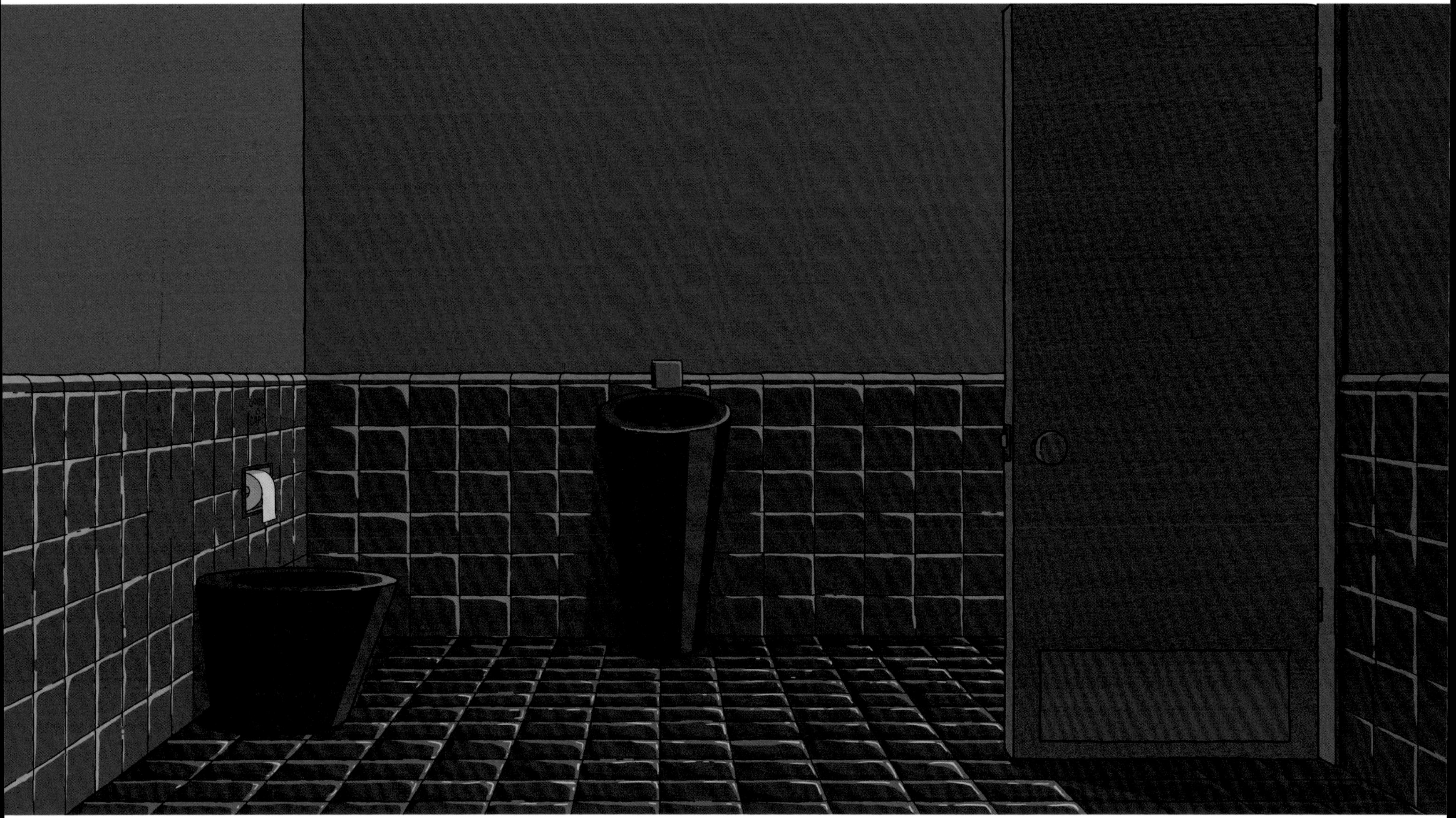

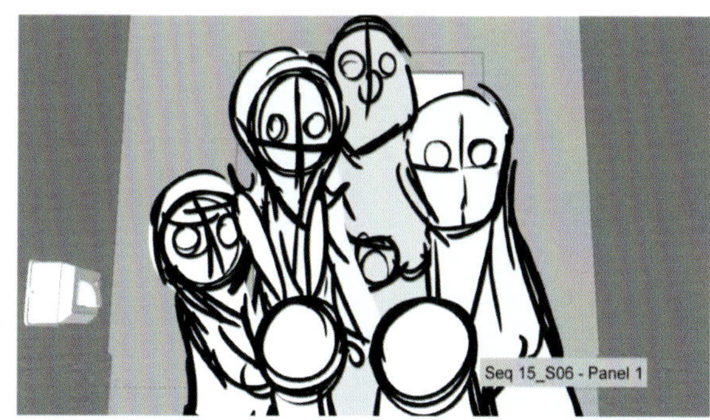

ABOVE:

BD: In the 100th episode, "Glued, Where's My Bob?", Bob gets stuck to the toilet. These "thumbnail" board panels show the family, Teddy, and Dr. Yap trying to pull Bob off the toilet before the crew from *Coasters* magazine arrives.

OPPOSITE:

LB: The incongruous and confusing restaurant bathroom forced on Bob and Linda by their landlord's younger brother, Felix, in the episode titled "Ambergris."

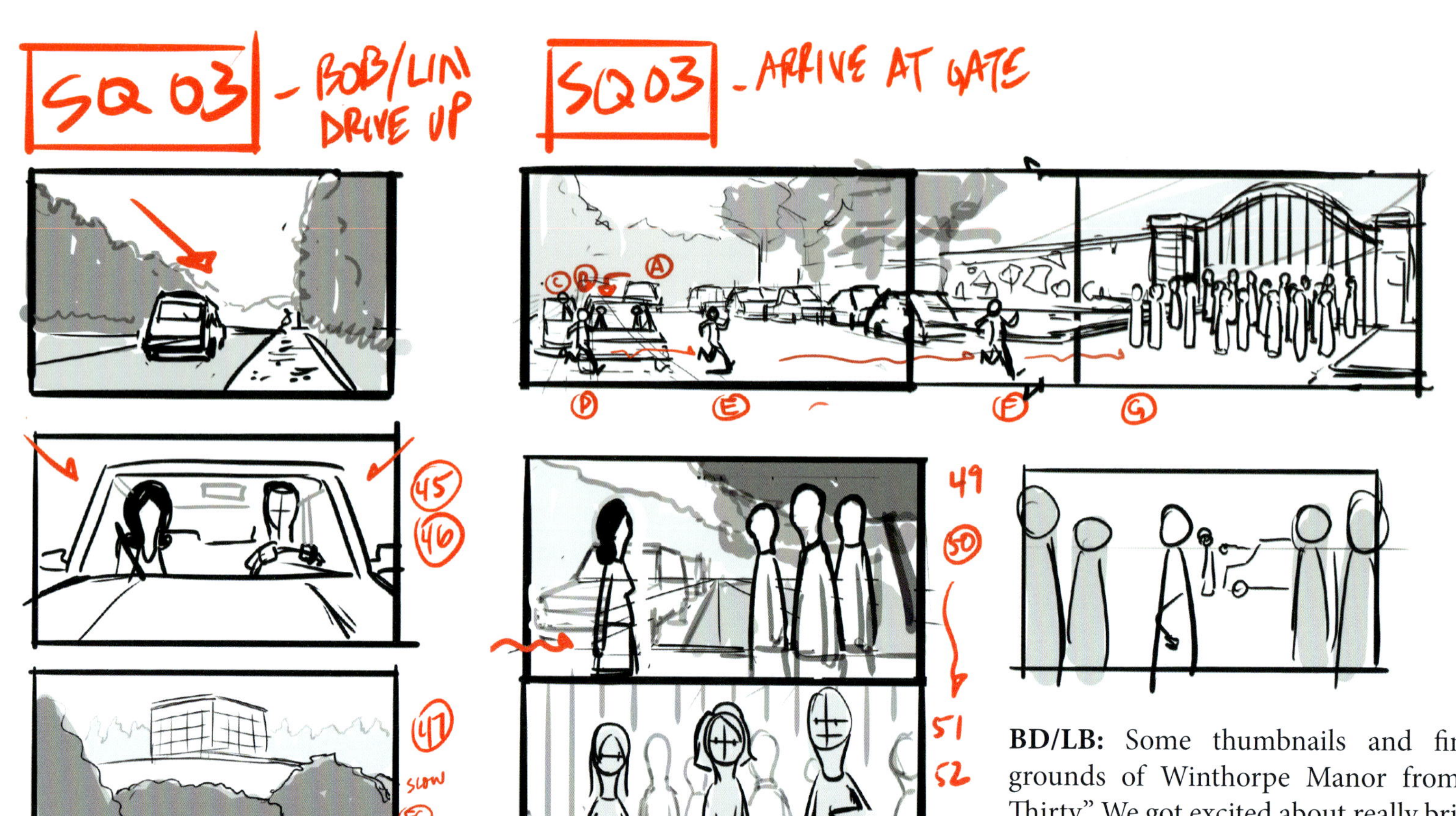

BD/LB: Some thumbnails and finished backgrounds of Winthorpe Manor from "Zero Larp Thirty." We got excited about really bringing out the opulence since it's a class warfare story and it's such a contrast to the Belchers' apartment. We also just love wallpaper and moulding.

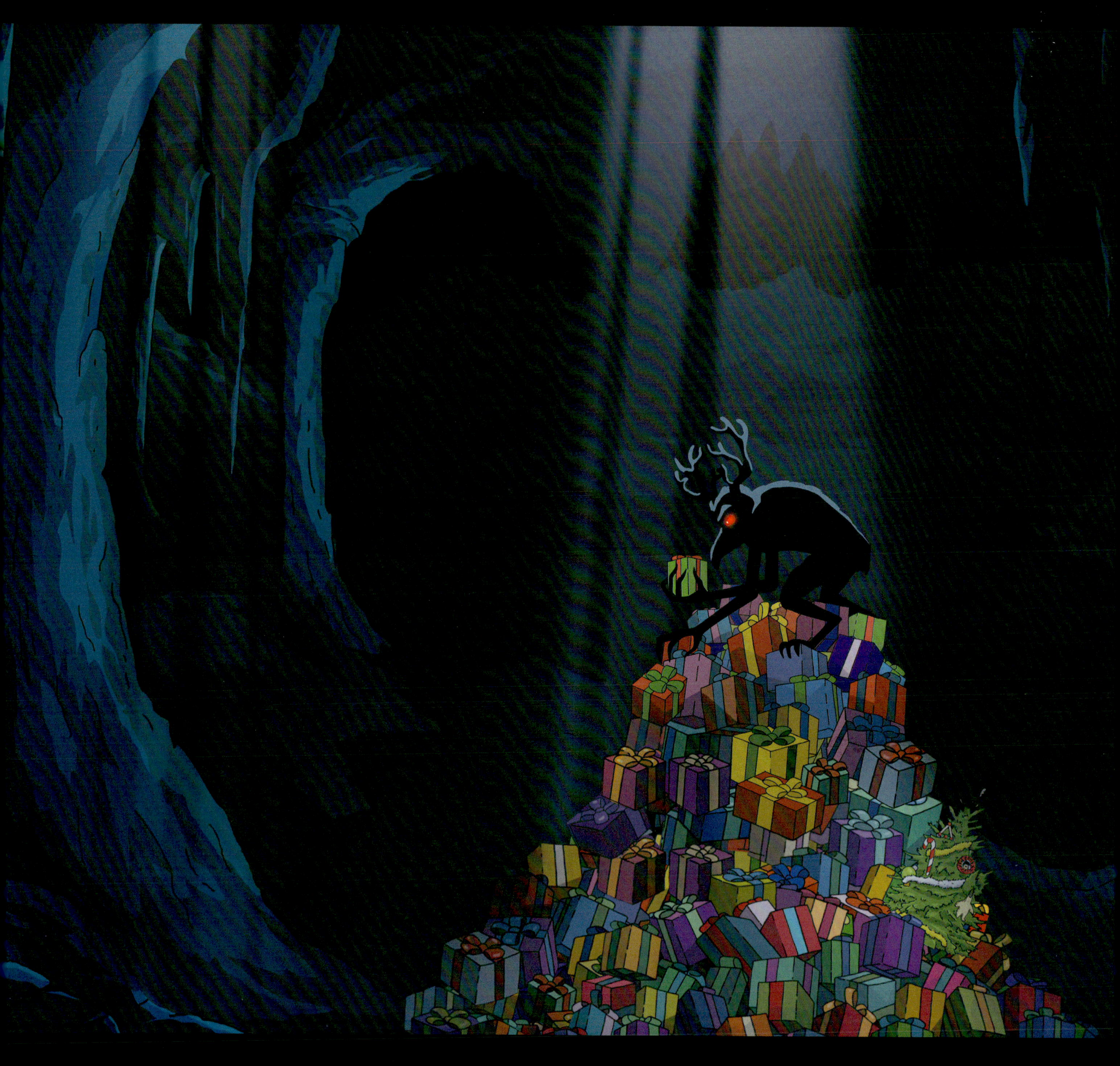

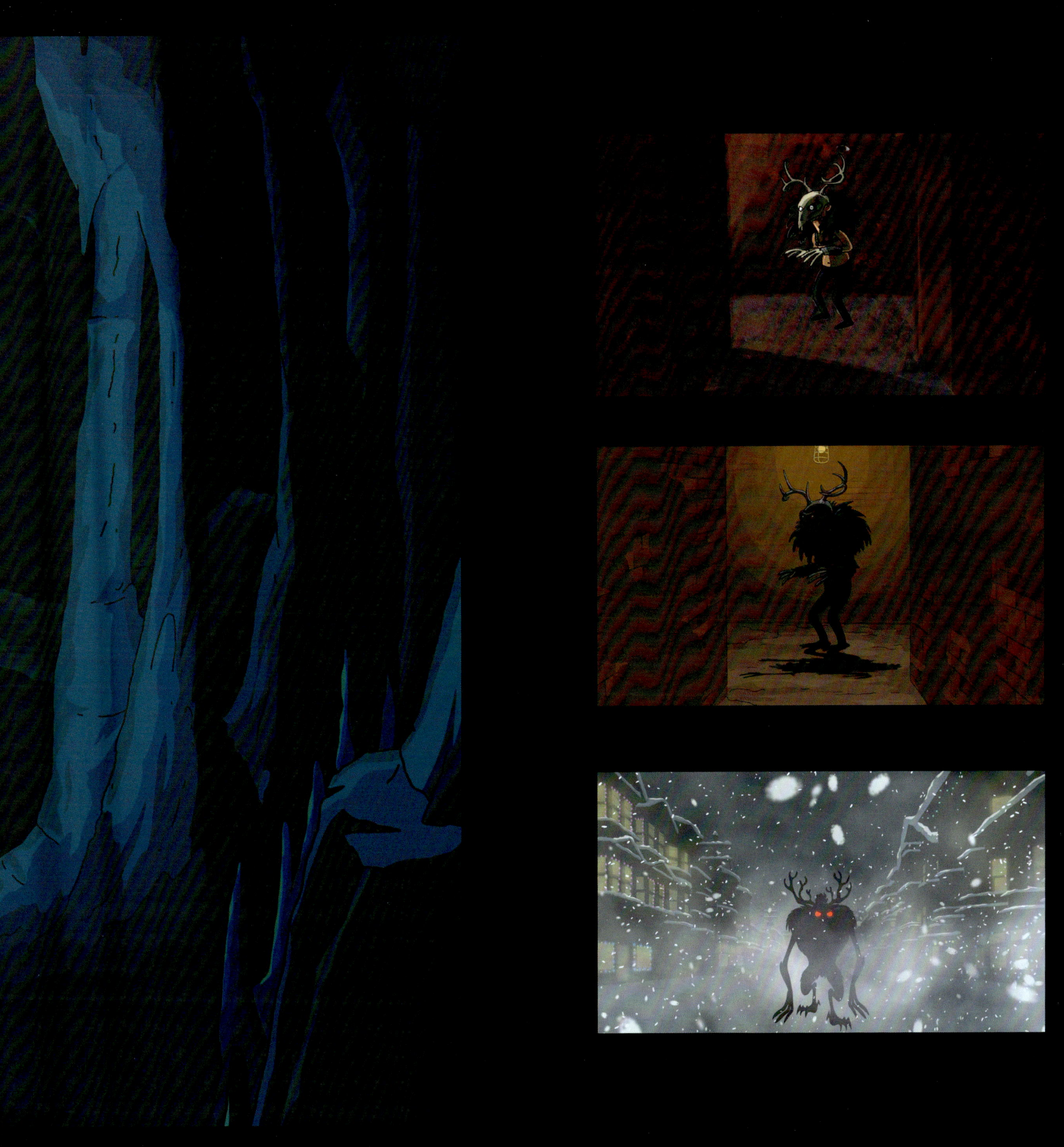

Panel 14

WONDER
WHARF

BOB'S BURGERS

ボブのバーガー屋

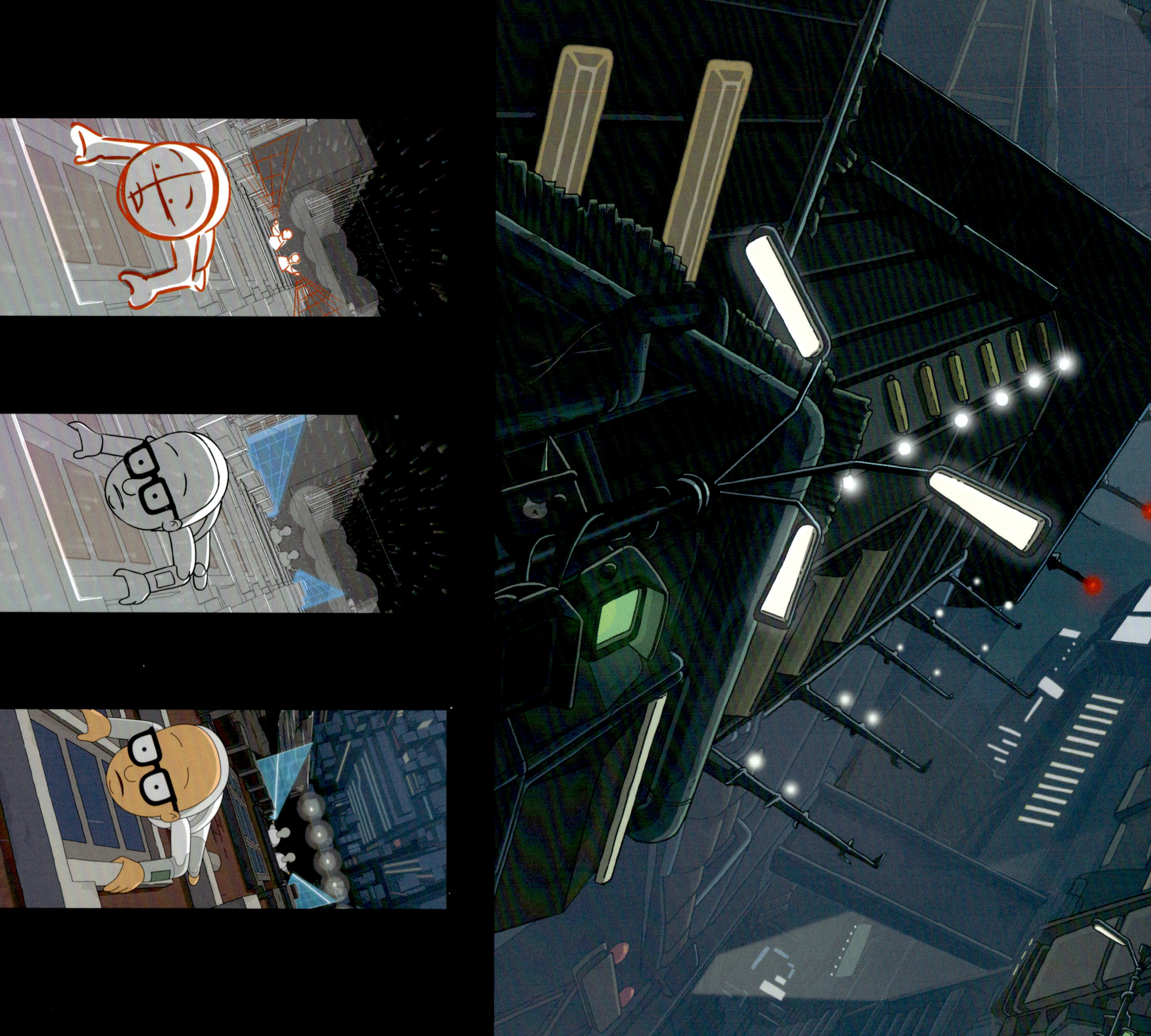

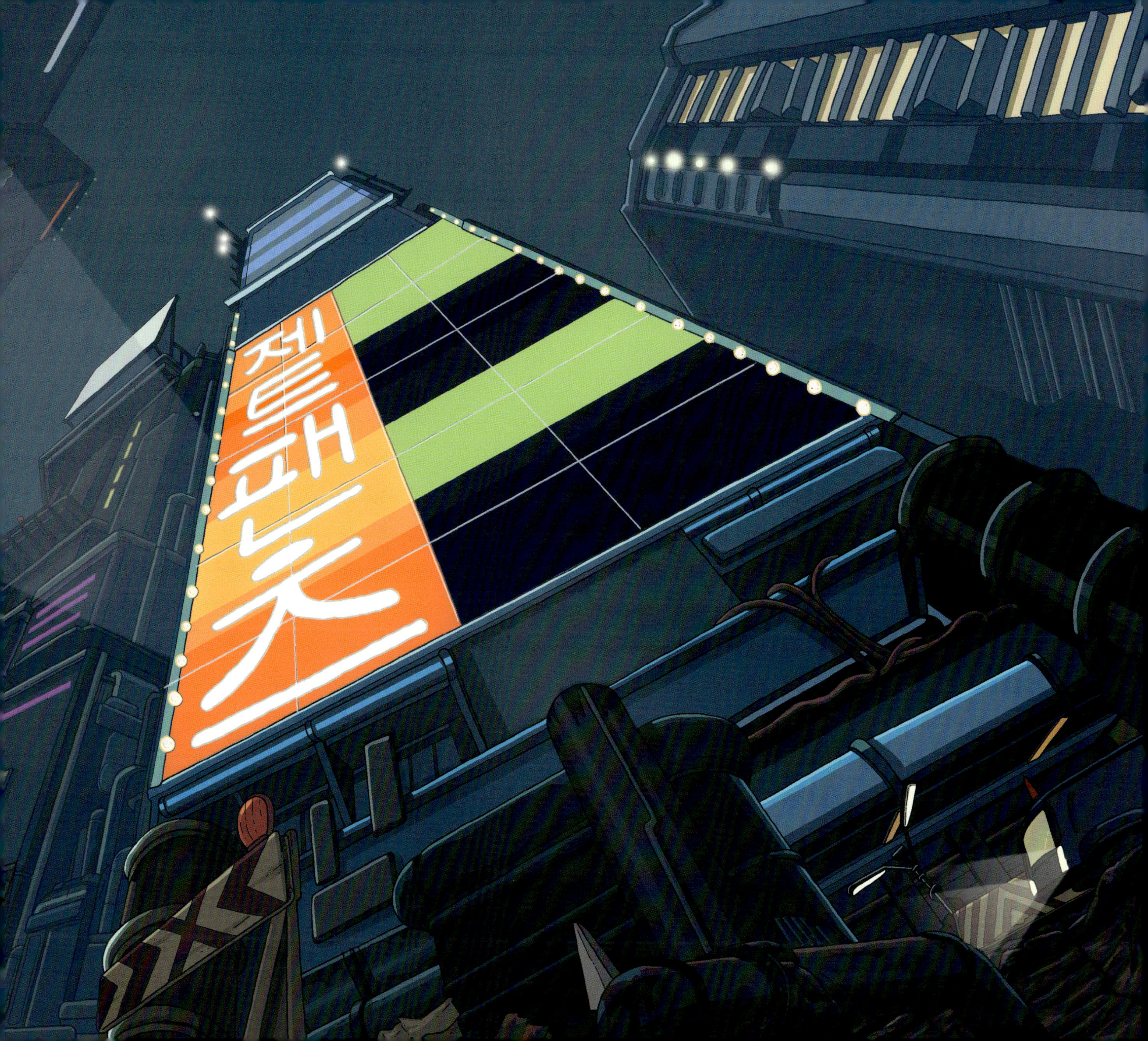

OFF
LIMITS

$5.00
REGULAR
$5.90
SPECIAL
ADD.50
CHEESE
$2.00
FRIES
$2.50
SIDE SALAD
$4.00
SOFT DRINK
$4.00
BEER

THE SCHOONER THE BETTER

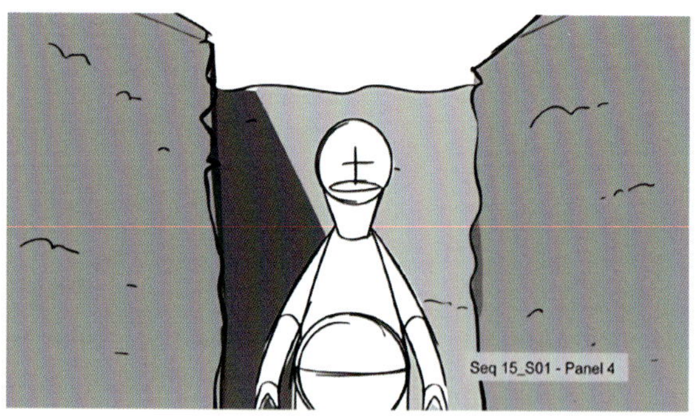

BD: THE ANIMATION PROCESS - Once the actors have been recorded and the audio has been edited, we begin the "thumb" process. The director and their storyboard team create rough drawings for all the shots in the episode, focusing on the staging and the length of the shots. This happens quickly; the director and team will complete the whole twenty-two-minute episode in a week.

BD: The thumbs are reviewed by the supervising director, the show-runners, and the writer of the episode. The next phase is called the "animatic." The same team builds on the thumb pass, adding more detail to the shots, and adding expression and posing for the characters. You can see here that a decision was made to delay the reveal of Mr. Fischoeder, and to add a close-up of Bob. The animatic process for each episode takes four weeks.

BD: The animatic is then screened for the whole studio, which gives everyone a chance to see how it plays for an audience. At this stage, the writers have an opportunity to do a small rewrite, and the storyboard team makes those changes to the animatic before it's shipped to the overseas animation studio along with detailed designs for every character, every prop, and every location. Lighting and time of day are carefully planned and "lip assignment" is prepared syllable by syllable, on an old-fashioned "X-sheet." Our overseas studios are in South Korea. There's a strong history of animation in Seoul and the teams are very talented. They bring the animatic to its next

stage, which we call “rough color.” In reality, it’s not rough at all: it looks very close to how it will look on air. The last phase is “post”—another screening, another rewrite, final picture “retakes,” final voice recording, then foley, sound effects, and music. From start to finish, it takes us approximately one year to make an episode.

FOLLOWING:
LB: Just a few of the incidental characters, or “incids,” that have appeared on *Bob’s*. We’ve grown fond of many of them.

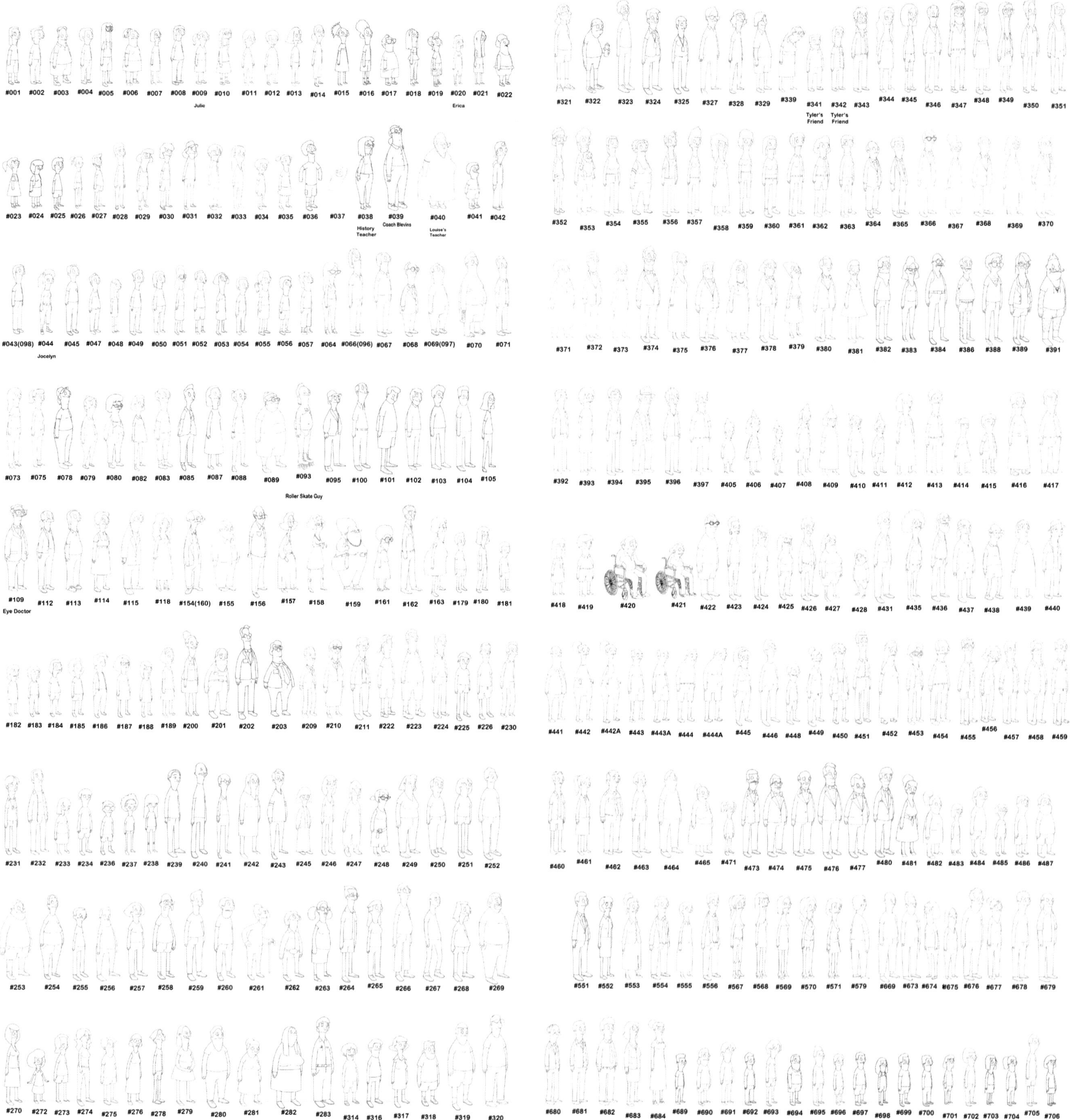
#001 #002 #003 #004 #005 #006 #007 #008 #009 #010 #011 #012 #013 #014 #015 #016 #017 #018 #019 #020 #021 #022
Julie
Erica
#023 #024 #025 #026 #027 #028 #029 #030 #031 #032 #033 #034 #035 #036 #037 #038 #039 #040 #041 #042
History Teacher
Coach Blevins
Louise's Teacher
#043(098) #044 #045 #047 #048 #049 #050 #051 #052 #053 #054 #055 #056 #057 #064 #066(096) #067 #068 #069(097) #070 #071
Jocelyn
#073 #075 #078 #079 #080 #082 #083 #085 #087 #088 #089 #093 #095 #100 #101 #102 #103 #104 #105
Roller Skate Guy
#109 #112 #113 #114 #115 #118 #154(160) #155 #156 #157 #158 #159 #161 #162 #163 #179 #180 #181
Eye Doctor
#182 #183 #184 #185 #186 #187 #188 #189 #200 #201 #202 #203 #209 #210 #211 #222 #223 #224 #225 #226 #230
#231 #232 #233 #234 #236 #237 #238 #239 #240 #241 #242 #243 #245 #246 #247 #248 #249 #250 #251 #252
#253 #254 #255 #256 #257 #258 #259 #260 #261 #262 #263 #264 #265 #266 #267 #268 #269
#270 #272 #273 #274 #275 #276 #278 #279 #280 #281 #282 #283 #314 #316 #317 #318 #319 #320
#321 #322 #323 #324 #325 #327 #328 #329 #339 #341 #342 #343 #344 #345 #346 #347 #348 #349 #350 #351
Tyler's Friend
Tyler's Friend
#352 #353 #354 #355 #356 #357 #358 #359 #360 #361 #362 #363 #364 #365 #366 #367 #368 #369 #370
#371 #372 #373 #374 #375 #376 #377 #378 #379 #380 #381 #382 #383 #384 #386 #388 #389 #391
#392 #393 #394 #395 #396 #397 #405 #406 #407 #408 #409 #410 #411 #412 #413 #414 #415 #416 #417
#418 #419 #420 #421 #422 #423 #424 #425 #426 #427 #428 #431 #435 #436 #437 #438 #439 #440
#441 #442 #442A #443 #443A #444 #444A #445 #446 #448 #449 #450 #451 #452 #453 #454 #455 #456 #457 #458 #459
#460 #461 #462 #463 #464 #465 #471 #473 #474 #475 #476 #477 #480 #481 #482 #483 #484 #485 #486 #487
#551 #552 #553 #554 #555 #556 #567 #568 #569 #570 #571 #579 #669 #673 #674 #675 #676 #677 #678 #679
#680 #681 #682 #683 #684 #689 #690 #691 #692 #693 #694 #695 #696 #697 #698 #699 #700 #701 #702 #703 #704 #705 #706

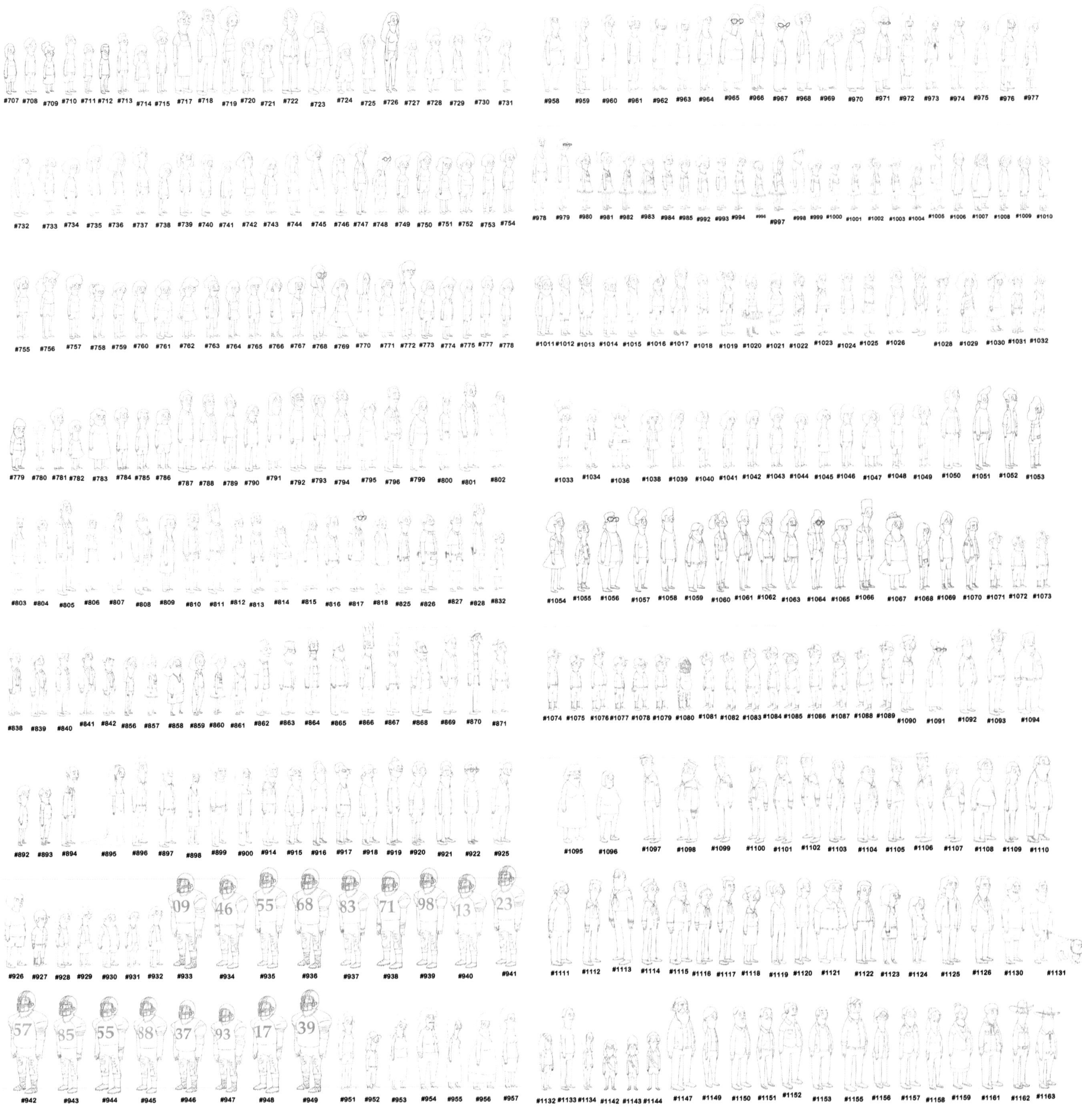
#707 #708 #709 #710 #711 #712 #713 #714 #715 #717 #718 #719 #720 #721 #722 #723 #724 #725 #726 #727 #728 #729 #730 #731
#958 #959 #960 #961 #962 #963 #964 #965 #966 #967 #968 #969 #970 #971 #972 #973 #974 #975 #976 #977
#732 #733 #734 #735 #736 #737 #738 #739 #740 #741 #742 #743 #744 #745 #746 #747 #748 #749 #750 #751 #752 #753 #754
#978 #979 #980 #981 #982 #983 #984 #985 #992 #993 #994 #996 #997 #998 #999 #1000 #1001 #1002 #1003 #1004 #1005 #1006 #1007 #1008 #1009 #1010
#755 #756 #757 #758 #759 #760 #761 #762 #763 #764 #765 #766 #767 #768 #769 #770 #771 #772 #773 #774 #775 #777 #778
#1011 #1012 #1013 #1014 #1015 #1016 #1017 #1018 #1019 #1020 #1021 #1022 #1023 #1024 #1025 #1026 #1028 #1029 #1030 #1031 #1032
#779 #780 #781 #782 #783 #784 #785 #786 #787 #788 #789 #790 #791 #792 #793 #794 #795 #796 #799 #800 #801 #802
#1033 #1034 #1036 #1038 #1039 #1040 #1041 #1042 #1043 #1044 #1045 #1046 #1047 #1048 #1049 #1050 #1051 #1052 #1053
#803 #804 #805 #806 #807 #808 #809 #810 #811 #812 #813 #814 #815 #816 #817 #818 #825 #826 #827 #828 #832
#1054 #1055 #1056 #1057 #1058 #1059 #1060 #1061 #1062 #1063 #1064 #1065 #1066 #1067 #1068 #1069 #1070 #1071 #1072 #1073
#838 #839 #840 #841 #842 #856 #857 #858 #859 #860 #861 #862 #863 #864 #865 #866 #867 #868 #869 #870 #871
#1074 #1075 #1076 #1077 #1078 #1079 #1080 #1081 #1082 #1083 #1084 #1085 #1086 #1087 #1088 #1089 #1090 #1091 #1092 #1093 #1094
#892 #893 #894 #895 #896 #897 #898 #899 #900 #914 #915 #916 #917 #918 #919 #920 #921 #922 #925
#1095 #1096 #1097 #1098 #1099 #1100 #1101 #1102 #1103 #1104 #1105 #1106 #1107 #1108 #1109 #1110
09 46 55 68 83 71 98 13 23
#926 #927 #928 #929 #930 #931 #932 #933 #934 #935 #936 #937 #938 #939 #940 #941
#1111 #1112 #1113 #1114 #1115 #1116 #1117 #1118 #1119 #1120 #1121 #1122 #1123 #1124 #1125 #1126 #1130 #1131
57 85 55 88 37 93 17 39
#942 #943 #944 #945 #946 #947 #948 #949 #951 #952 #953 #954 #955 #956 #957
#1132 #1133 #1134 #1142 #1143 #1144 #1147 #1149 #1150 #1151 #1152 #1153 #1155 #1156 #1157 #1158 #1159 #1161 #1162 #1163

BUROBU
ブロブ
ブロブ
BUROBU

RUPUNZ-SLUG
STAGE 3
14 HP
BUROBU

LITTLE RED RIDING SLUG
STAGE 2
24HP
BUROBU

JACK AND THE BEAN SLUG
STAGE 2
47 HP
BUROBU

SNOW SLUG AND THE SEVEN SLUGS
STAGE 3
75 HP
BUROBU

SLUG IN BOOTS
STAGE 1
19 HP
BUROBU

SLUG-ERELLA
STAGE 2
41 HP
BUROBU

RUMPLE SLUG-SKIN
STAGE 1
30HP
BUROBU

THE SLUGGITIVE
STAGE 9
93HP
BUROBU

BUROBU
MAGAZINE

SLUGDOZER
SLUGCAVATOR
SLUGGY SLUGBORNE
SLUGATHA CHRISTIE
SLUGTRIFUGE
COYOTE SLUGLY
SLUGGER
SLUGIGATOR
SLUGCUPATIONAL THERAPIST
BUROBU
MASH MISSILE
Slug-I-Cane
POWER PACK
BUROBU
TRADING CARD GAME
LEAGUE
Spring Release

SLUGODACTYL
STAGE 4
48 HP
BUROBU

SLUGODACTYL
STAGE 5
57 HP
BUROBU

SLUGODACTYL
STAGE 6
65 HP
BUROBU

SLUGODACTYL
STAGE 7
78 HP
BUROBU

SLUGODACTYL
STAGE 8
82 HP
BUROBU

SLUGODACTYL
STAGE 9
99 HP
BUROBU

SLUGICOPTER
STAGE 3
38 HP
BUROBU

SLUGCANO
STAGE 1
35 HP
BUROBU

SLUGCANO
STAGE 2
41 HP
BUROBU

SLUGCANO
STAGE 3
53 HP
BUROBU

SLUGCANO
STAGE 9
99 HP
BUROBU

SLUGCLOPS
STAGE 1
26 HP
BUROBU

SLUGCLOPS
STAGE 7
79 HP
BUROBU

SLUGVERTIBLE
STAGE 4
45 HP
BUROBU

SLUG ARMY KNIFE
STAGE 1
9 HP
BUROBU

SLUG ARMY KNIFE
STAGE 3
37 HP
BUROBU

SLUG ARMY KNIFE
STAGE 6
65 HP
BUROBU

SLUG ARMY KNIFE
STAGE 7
79 HP
BUROBU

SLUGTOPUS
STAGE 1
13 HP
BUROBU

SLUGTOPUS
STAGE 3
39 HP
BUROBU

SLUGSAPHONE
STAGE 6
48 HP
BUROBU

BUROBU
BUROBU

MEGA ULTRA
SLUGITTARIUS
STAGE
BUROBU

MEGA ULTRA
SLUGCANO
STAGE
BUROBU

MEGA ULTRA
SLUGERANTULA
STAGE
BUROBU

MEGA ULTRA MACHO
SLUGMARINE
STAGE
BUROBU

ADDITIONAL ART

LB: When were still a young show, a publisher called Dynamite asked us if wanted to make a comic book, and we said "Yes!" way too loudly. Many of the artists who work on the show used the comic book to stretch the style. We were very inspired by the fan art we were seeing online. We even licensed some of it and featured it in the comic book.

DYNAMITE

BOB'S BURGERS

AIT, AREN'T YOU GOING
, LIKE, MELT INTO A
ILE OF GOOP OR SOMETHING?
SINCE YOU'RE AN ALIEN?
YOU'RE NOT?
Oh. Sorry. I thought you were an alien.
FIN
HOW TO
EAT HIM
ECAMERA!

SAVING MR SHANKS BURGER
with lamb shanks)
$5.95
Let's go inside and make a fort out of COUCH CUSHIONS!!!
Kat Kosmala 2014
FIN

Tina's Erotic Friend Fiction Presents:
Omega
Tina
MY NAME IS TINA BELCHER AND I AM THE LAST PERSON ON EARTH. WHICH IS NOT GREAT, BUT IT ISN'T AS BAD AS IT SOUNDS.
It's your
crematorium
IT'S THE END OF THE WORLD AS WE KNOW IT AND I NEED LINE - FISHING SUPPLY STORE
ON THE PLUS SIDE, I GET PLENTY OF ME TIME. OF COURSE, I DO GET LONELY.
OH YEAH. THERE ARE ZOMBIES TOO. 14 TO 16 YEAR OLD BOY ZOMBIES.
BUT THEY KEPT TRYING TO EAT ME...

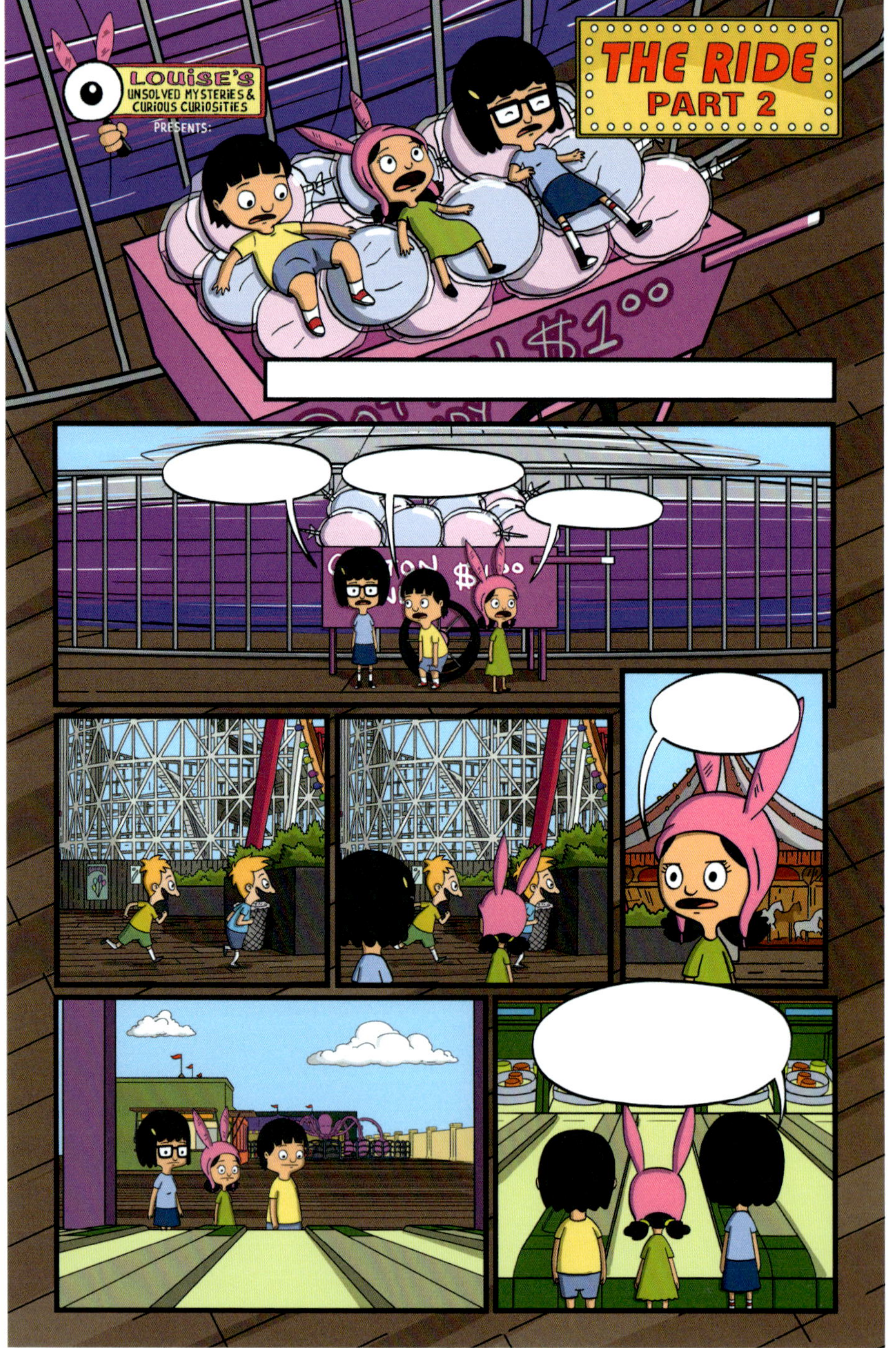
LOUISE'S UNSOLVED MYSTERIES & CURIOUS CURIOSITIES
PRESENTS:
THE RIDE
PART 2
$1.00

LOUISE'S UNSOLVED MYSTERIES & CURIOUS CURIOSITIES

WHO FORTED?

it's BEAUTIFUL!

I GUESS IT IS KIND OF BEAUTIFUL. I MEAN, AS FREEZERS GO.

No, the box. Can we have it?

OH. YEAH, YOU CAN HAVE THE BOX.

IT'S A PRETTY NICE FREEZER, THOUGH, FYI.

GUYS guess what we're going to do with THIS!

Start a breakdancing troupe?

Recycle?

REBUILD THE FORT!

If you guys want boxes, I have a friend at a hardware store who's always getting rid of them.

YES!!

How many do you want?

ALL OF THEM!

LATER...

My room has a walk-in closet!

My room has a COZY window seat for quiet contemplation

My room has a TOILET BED!

O'S
BOB'S BUR

DEREK
SCHROEDER
2015

BELCHER RACING

DEREK
SCHROEDER
2015

PESTO

MILK

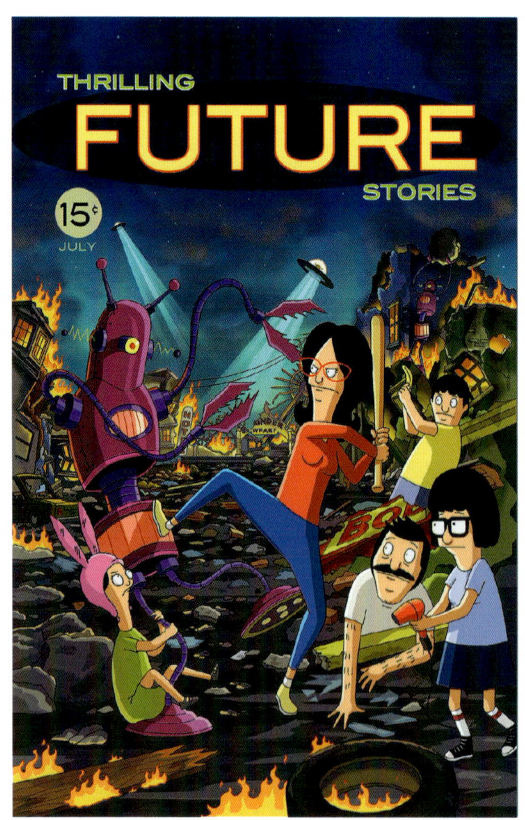

THRILLING
FUTURE
STORIES
15¢
JULY

BURGER OF THE DAY
THE HARRY POUTINE-Y BURGER
$5.95

KAA

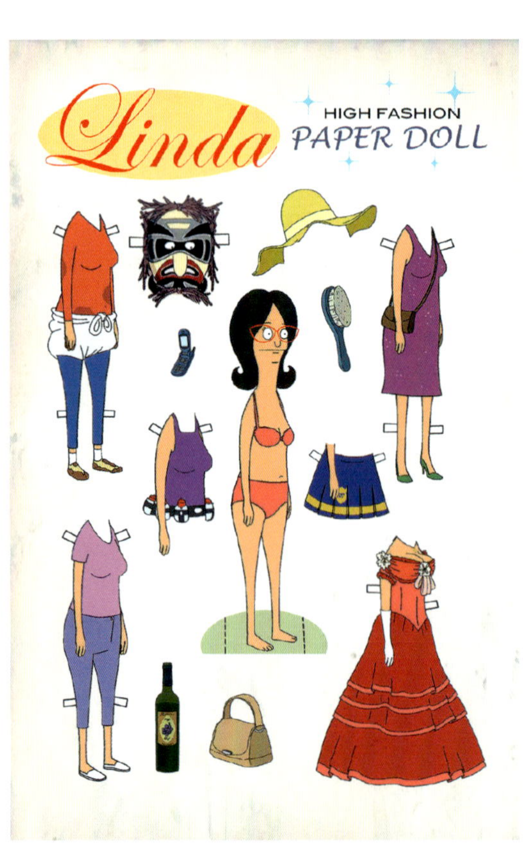
Linda
HIGH FASHION
PAPER DOLL

BOB'S BURGERS

Uhhh

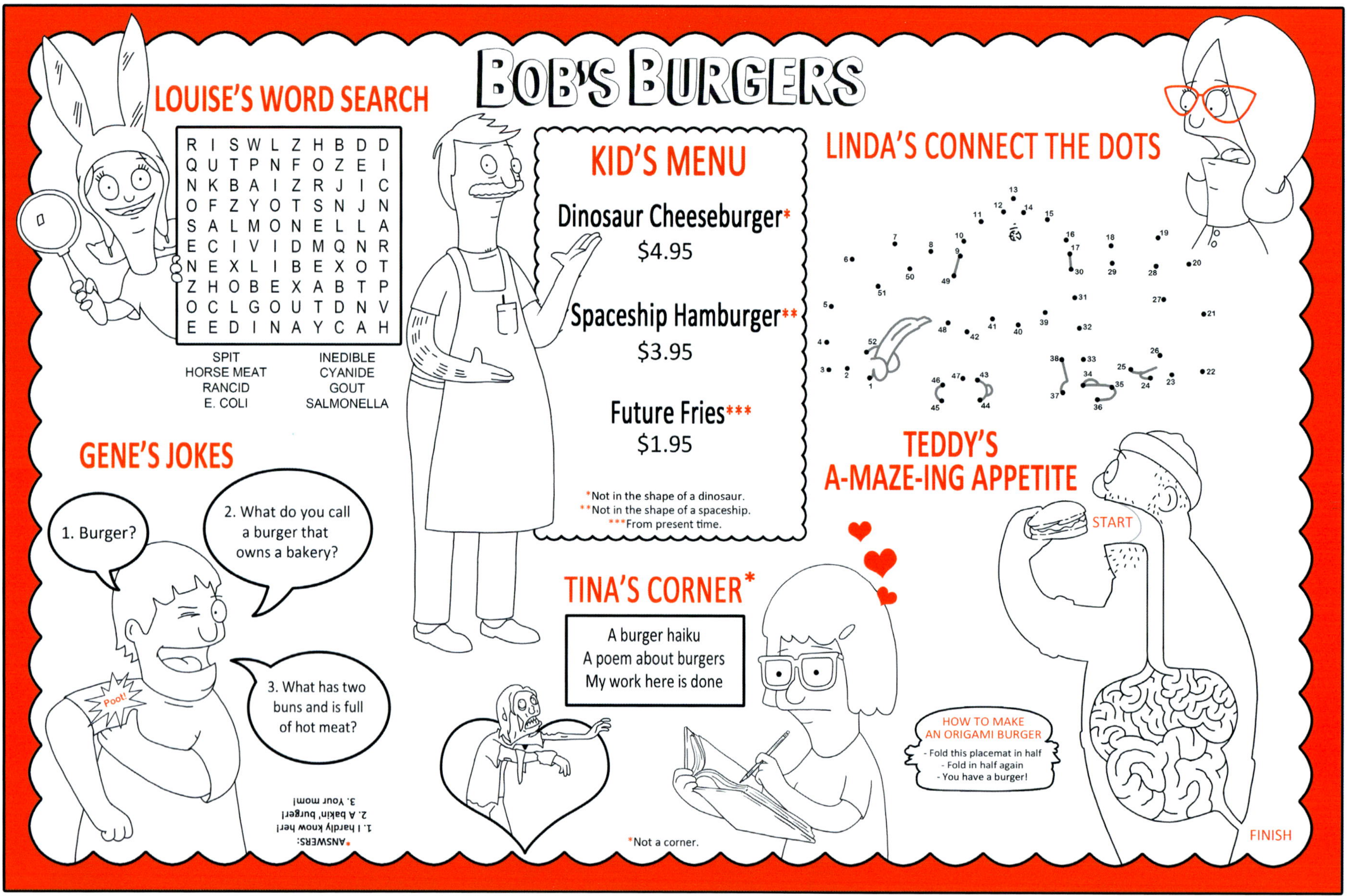

LB: Comic Con has always been special for us. We make a new, exclusive poster every year to sign and give away to fans. We like them, too. We frame them and put them up in our studio.

POST THIS IN A HIGHLY VISIBLE AREA

CHOKING FIRST AID

IN AN EMERGENCY CALL 911

CONSCIOUS VICTIM STANDING

1 RECOGNIZE CHOKING SIGNS

Choking victim will have trouble speaking, coughing, and of course, breathing. Victim may be dramatically clutching his throat as if to say, "hey, everybody look at me, look at me." Cross your arms and firmly tell the victim that you won't help him until he stops being such a diva.

2 IF CHOKING – APPLY ABDOMINAL THRUSTS

Stand behind the victim. Wrap your arms around his waist. Whisper in his ear "you're gonna owe me big," then make a fist, place it above the tummy hole and below the bosom cage. Grab this fist with your other hand. Press inward and upward with 5 quick thrusts while repeating the phrase " I'm a hero." Continue these thrusts until the object comes out or until you get distracted by something else.

3 IF PREGNANT OR OBESE – APPLY CHEST THRUSTS

If the victim is pregnant, compliment her on her full breasts. If the victim is obese, same thing. Then make your hand into a fist, wave it in their face, and say "usually when you see this, it means trouble," then grab the fist with your other hand and apply five quick thrusts. Be sure to tell the pregnant victim your name so that she knows what to call her baby.

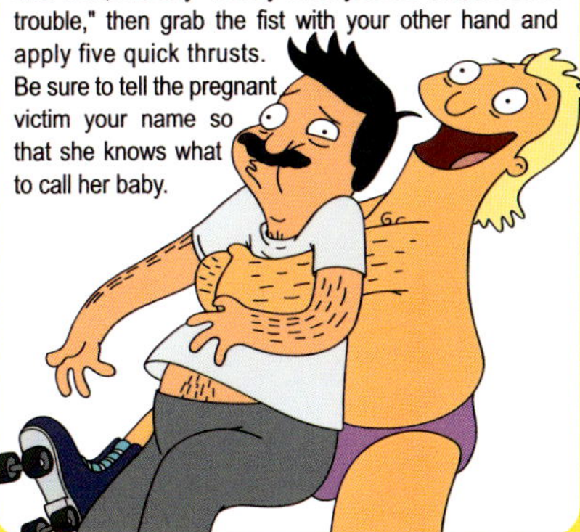

VICTIM LYING CONSCIOUS OR UNCONSCIOUS

1 CHECK TO SEE IF CONSCIOUS OR UNCONSCIOUS

Gently shake the victim's shoulders to find out if he is okay. If the victim doesn't respond, shout loudly that his pants are pulled down and you can see EVERYTHING. If the victim still doesn't respond, pretend that you are going to leave and not help them. If they still don't respond proceed to step 2.

2 POSITION VICTIM ON BACK

If the victim is lying face down, first say "very funny, wise guy." Then take a firm grip of the victim's mustache, love handles, and/or groin, and roll him over. Take a long look at him to see how attractive he is. Don't forget to take personality into account.

3 OPEN THE AIRWAY FOR BREATHING

Apply downward pressure on the victim's forehead and lift his chin. If the chin is dimpled, put your finger in the dimple and say "honk." Then make your finger into a deep sea diver and imagine the victim's throat is the underwater cavern you must go down into to find the food treasure before the Russians get it. Take the plunge.

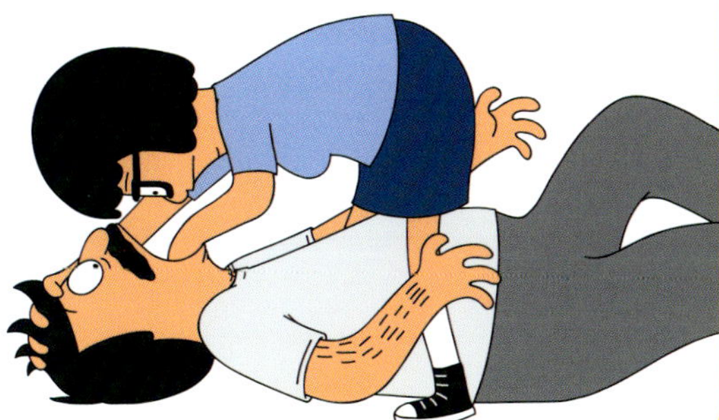

4 ATTEMPT MOUTH TO MOUTH

Keeping the head tilted and the mouth open, pinch the victim's nose to make him look more elegant, then say "all aboard the smooch train,"and place your lips over his. Firmly but sensually blow into his mouth. If the victim feels like you are not into it, he is less likely to start breathing again. If the victim feels like you are too into it, just tell him he's not special - that's how you kiss everybody.

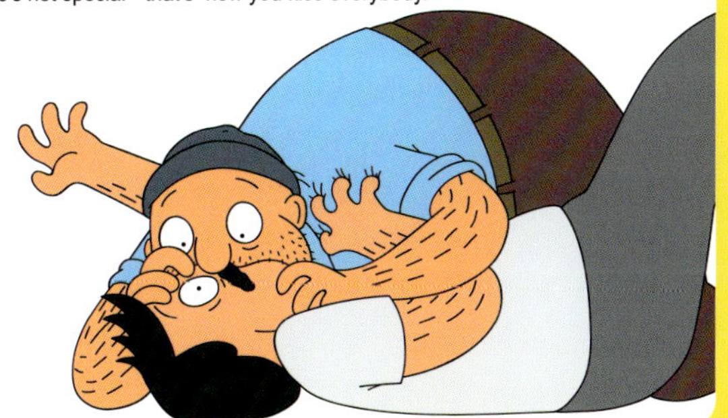

Disclaimer: These instructions are meant for entertainment purposes only. In the event of a real emergency, please contact 9-1-1.

BOB'S BURGERS
FOOD PYRAMID
BURGERS
The tip. The top. The complete package. Burgers are the window to the soul of your eyes' stomachs. This is just a fact.
PROTEIN
Basically, the meat part of the burger. Yeah, there's fish, nuts, beans… Ignore them! What are you gonna do, eat a salmon? How ridiculous does that sound? Eat a burger. Done.
GRAINS
This means bread, also known as a bun. It holds a burger. Why are you still not eating one? Fix it!
VEGETABLES
Lettuce, onions, pickles. Those are vegetables. Where's a good place to find those? Hmmm. Why can't I think of it? It's not on a burger is it? It is? Okay, yeah. That's what I was gonna say.
FRUITS
If you wanna get technical, a tomato is a fruit. Look it up. Seriously, look it up. You see where this is going right? Okay, now put down your dictionary and just go to the top of the pyramid and get everything in one place.
DAIRY
Cheese. Is there such a thing as a cheeseburger? A magical thing called a cheeseburger??? There is!?! That's amazing. Was it sent here by aliens? Sorry. We've had about eighteen burgers today. We're gonna go take a nap.
This food pyramid has not been approved by the FDA, the EPA, the FBI, the CIA, the AARP or your parents. But we're not all hung up on approval. I mean, it's great to feel validated. But we're working on just feeling really centered and focused and happy doing our own thing.

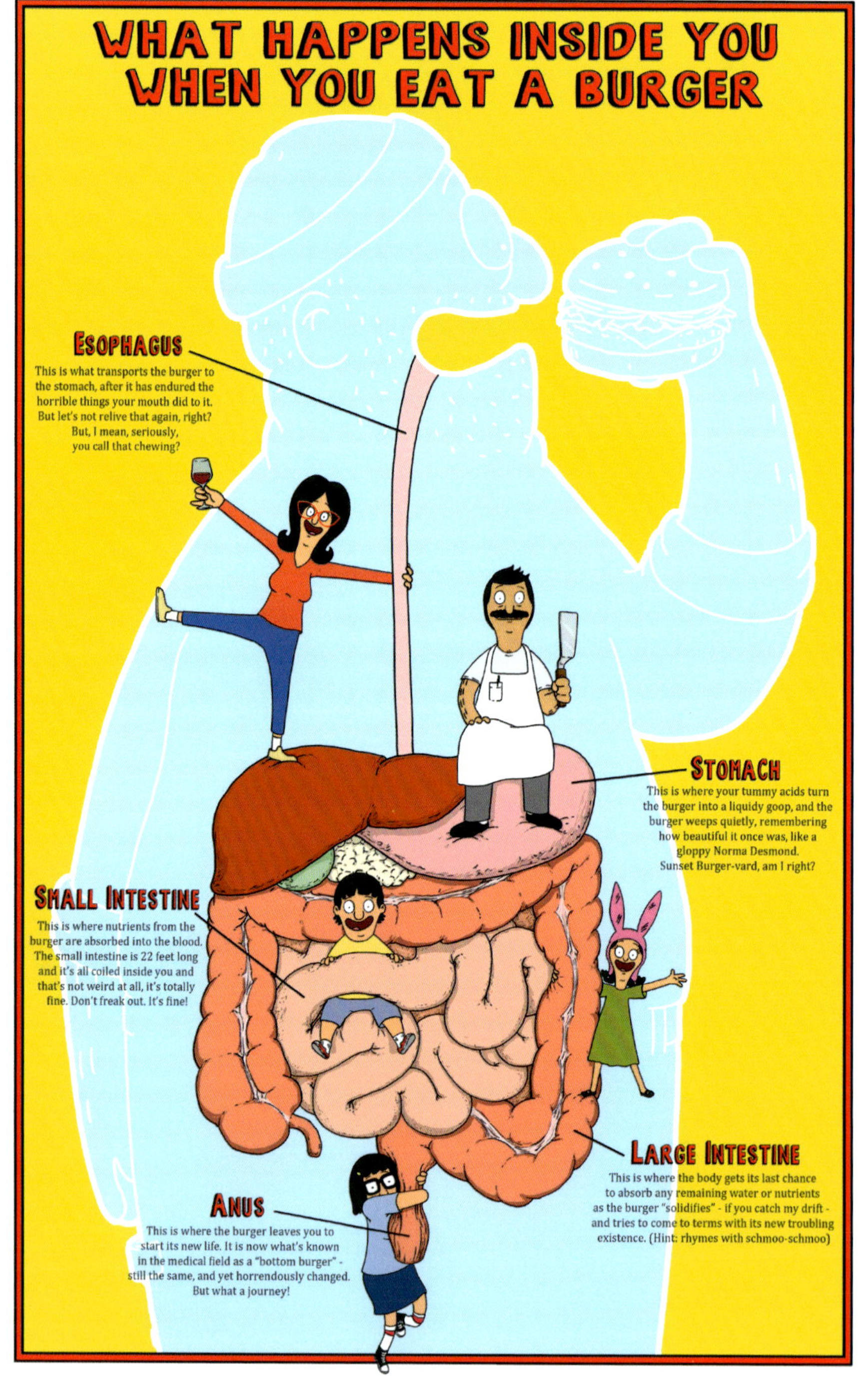
WHAT HAPPENS INSIDE YOU WHEN YOU EAT A BURGER
ESOPHAGUS
This is what transports the burger to the stomach, after it has endured the horrible things your mouth did to it. But let's not relive that again, right? But, I mean, seriously, you call that chewing?
STOMACH
This is where your tummy acids turn the burger into a liquidy goop, and the burger weeps quietly, remembering how beautiful it once was, like a gloppy Norma Desmond. Sunset Burger-vard, am I right?
SMALL INTESTINE
This is where nutrients from the burger are absorbed into the blood. The small intestine is 22 feet long and it's all coiled inside you and that's not weird at all, it's totally fine. Don't freak out. It's fine!
LARGE INTESTINE
This is where the body gets its last chance to absorb any remaining water or nutrients as the burger "solidifies" - if you catch my drift - and tries to come to terms with its new troubling existence. (Hint: rhymes with schmoo-schmoo)
ANUS
This is where the burger leaves you to start its new life. It is now what's known in the medical field as a "bottom burger" - still the same, and yet horrendously changed. But what a journey!

BURGER YOGA
BLOSSOMING LOTUS POSE WITH BURGER
Blossoming Lotus Pose opens your hips and chest, develops your core muscles, increases your balance, strengthens your arms, and is a great way to greet house guests.
HOW TO DO:
Sit on your bottom and put the soles of your feet together like they're giving each other a foot high five. Lift your legs up and weave your arms under your legs so that you look like a blossoming lotus or a drunk crab or someone that wants to look at their own butt. Hold the burger in your right hand and try not to get any foot on it.
GARLAND POSE WITH BURGER
Garland pose stretches the ankles, back, and groin and is guaranteed to rip all of your pants.
HOW TO DO:
Squat with your feet as close together as possible. At this point your pants have ripped. Separate your thighs and press outward with your elbows against your knees.
Think about the new pair of pants you're going to buy.
These will be better. These will last. Bring your palms together, and of course, there should be a burger on your head.
TREE POSE WITH BURGER
Tree pose establishes strength and balance and will make you wonder how trees do it all day.
HOW TO DO:
Stand with your legs together, just like you do sometimes. Bend your left knee and raise your left foot, placing the sole of it on your inner right thigh, just like a tree does. Hold your burger in both hands but don't eat it because we're not eating burgers right now, we're doing yoga WITH burgers. There's a difference.
DOWNWARD-FACING DOG POSE WITH BURGER
Downward-Facing Dog pose is the ultimate all-over stretch and is the best pose for showing your dog he's not that special, anyone can do what he does.
HOW TO DO:
Get down on your hands and knees. If your dog is there, make strong eye contact with him. Who's the dog now? Exhale and lift your knees away from the floor. Did you remember to put a burger on your butt? If you didn't, figure it out. Don't embarrass yourself in front of your dog.
WARRIOR 2 POSE WITH BURGER
Warrior 2 pose is like the Warrior 1 pose but if you have to go number 2. This pose opens up the hips and the groin, slaps them in the face, and says "Snap out of it!"
HOW TO DO:
Stand with your feet one human leg's length apart. Stretch your arms out, holding the burger in your dominant hand. If an enemy approaches, pretend you're gonna throw the burger at them. But don't actually throw the burger.
You want to eat that burger.
HAPPY BABY POSE WITH BURGER
Happy Baby Pose brings a greater awareness to the hip joints and also celebrates the one thing babies are known for being good at - grabbing their dumb feet.
HOW TO DO:
Lie on your back. Bend your knees to your stomach and grab your feet. Pull your knees up into your armpits - which is something neither will see coming. Make sure you've placed a burger on your butt. Otherwise the whole thing is pointless.

BURGER BALL
10
10
100
SURPRISE INSPECTION
FLIPPER
FLIPPER
ZOOM
- PULL THE SPRINGY STICK ON THE RIGHT
- SHOOT A BALL UP. PEW!
- USE FLIPPERS TO KEEP BALL HAPPY.
- FREE PLAY AT WHAT, 100,000 POINTS? 1,000,000? LET'S SAY 1,000,000
- FOR AMUSEMENT MOSTLY. COOL. COOL.
DON'T TIIIILLLT!
BALLS PLAYED
25¢
1 PLAY

CAFFREY'S Taffy
DANGER KEEP OUT
the Ear Drum
PATRICIA'S 77 SANDWICHES
KIM & SON'S HARDWARE
JUST STOW
MR. GRAVY PAWS
"The most stuff you can grind up to make food"

WONDER WHARF
TOUCH N' SEA AQUARIUM
Family FUNTIME
GLENCREST YACHT CLUB
FERRY ENTRANCE
Spare Change Lanes
BOWL
HOTEL
BUS
TOP HAT CINEMA
Hair Barrel
SHOW ME YOUR BADGE BADGER REMOVAL
OMG MALL
fig jam
Waxing Philosophical
Capoeira CENTER FOR CAPOEIRA
Great Escape-tations
ABOUT A TOY
Petrorama
WAGSTAFF
WELCOME TO
Seymour's Bay
NEXT 3 EXITS
ELEGANT DOILY RETIREMENT HOME
The Hobby Hole
REGGIE'S DELI
OPEN
BOB'S BURGERS
Accurate* and Definitive** Map*** of Seymour's Bay****
*Map is not accurate. **Map is not definitive. ***Map isn't so much a MAP as like a "map". ****Technically might not be a bay.

BIG BOB'S
DINER

LB: Promotional images have a special job to do and, with very few exceptions, we try to make sure they come out of our shop and are retouched by our most senior artists. We like everyone to be "in character" and "on model."

BOB'S BURGERS

1

LB: Sometimes a recording artist, such as The National, will cover one of our songs, and when that happens, we like to make an animated music video ("Bob's Buskers"). As you can imagine, this is both really fun and much harder than you think it's going to be when you start. We try to make each one as close to a work of art as we can. Music and animation are special friends.

ABOVE: The National.
OPPOSITE: The National and (*lower right*) Låpsley.

BIG GIRLS DON'T DRY CLEANERS

St. Vincent

Sleater - Kinney

Stephin Merritt and Kenny Mellman

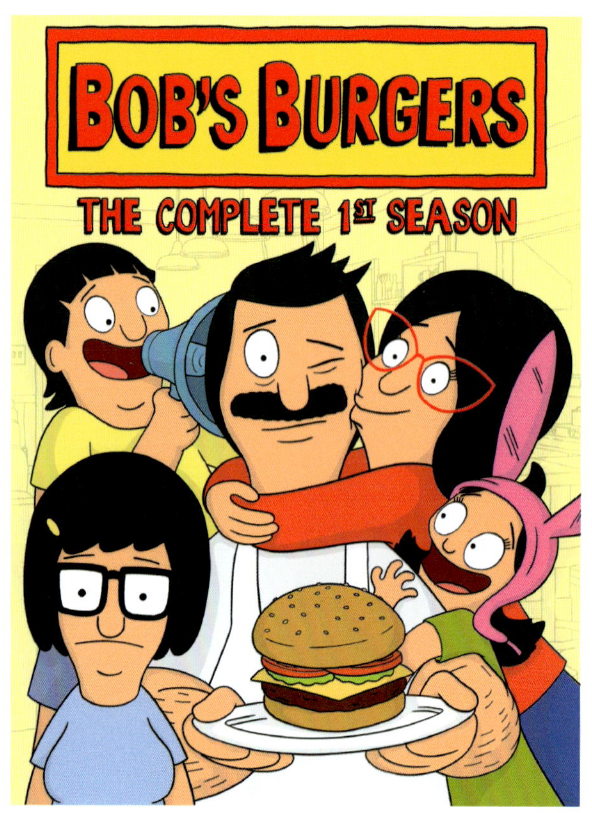

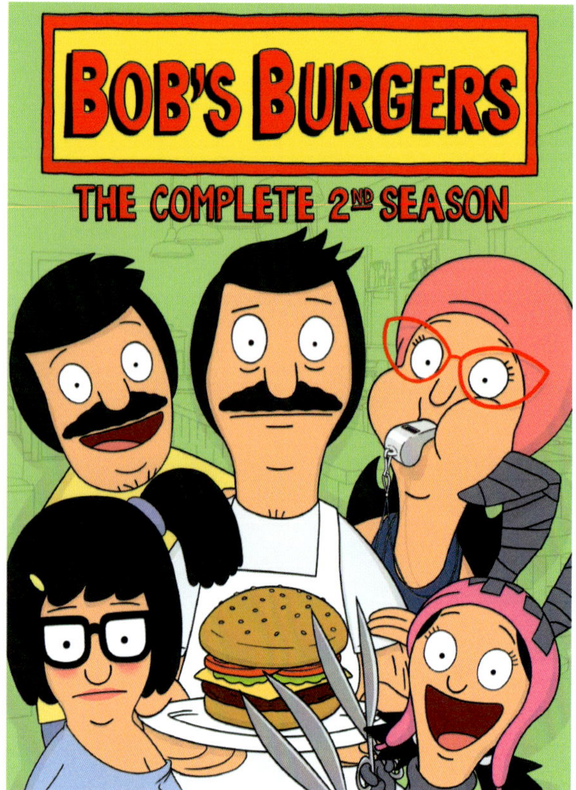

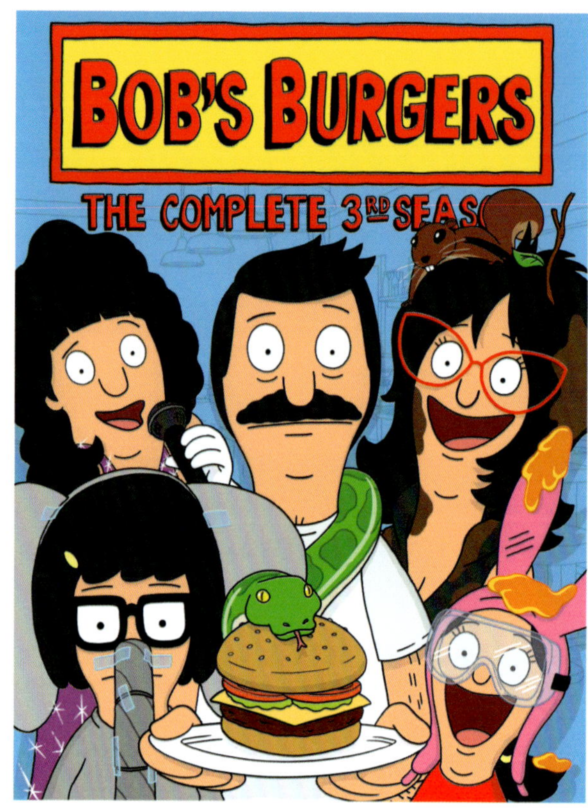

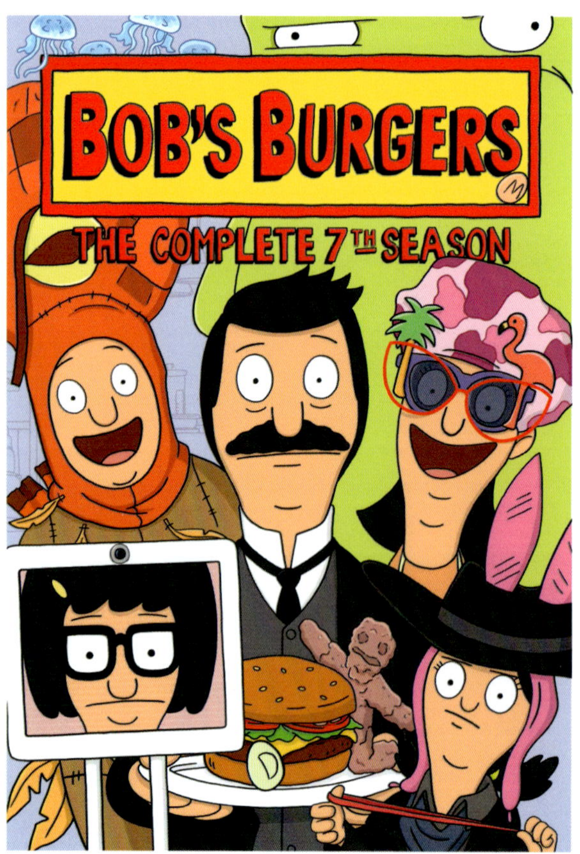

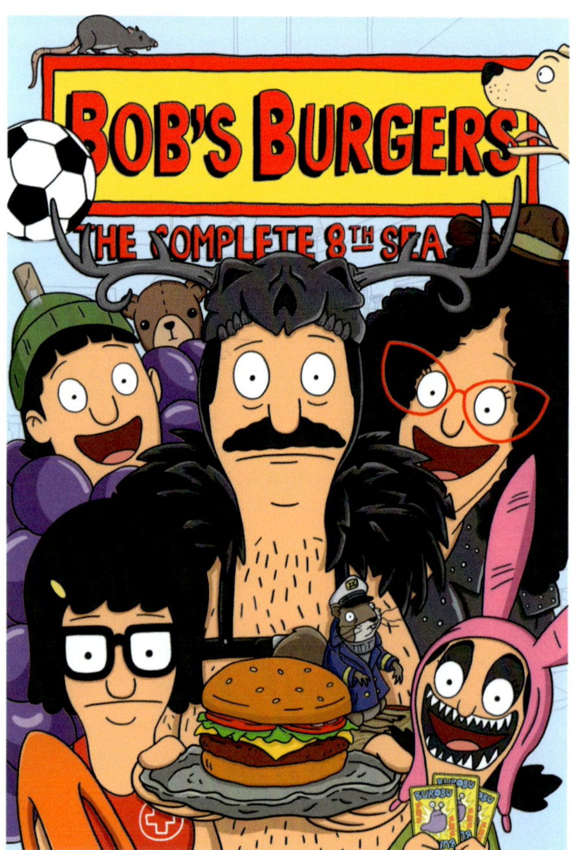

LB: Remember DVDs? We used to make them, and each season got its own custom cover.

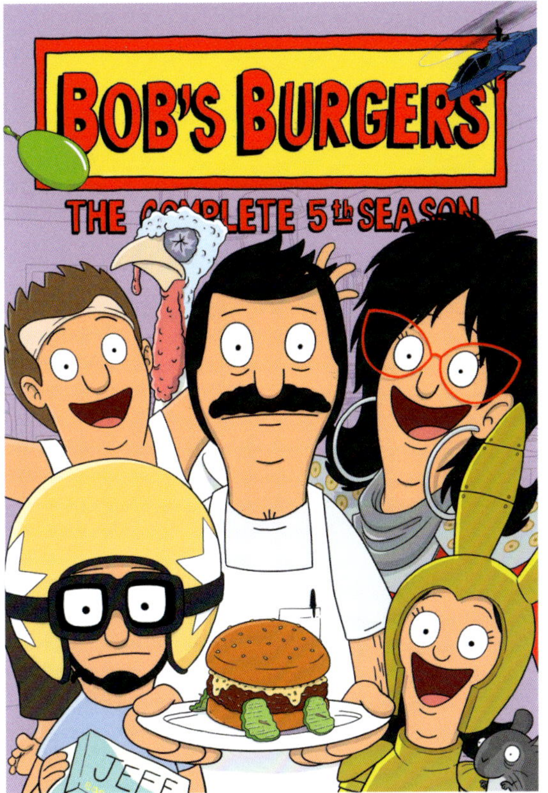

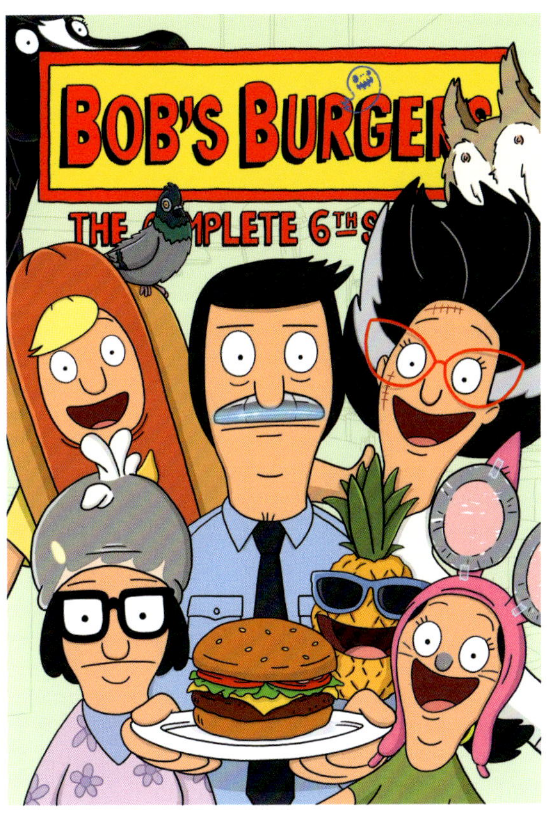

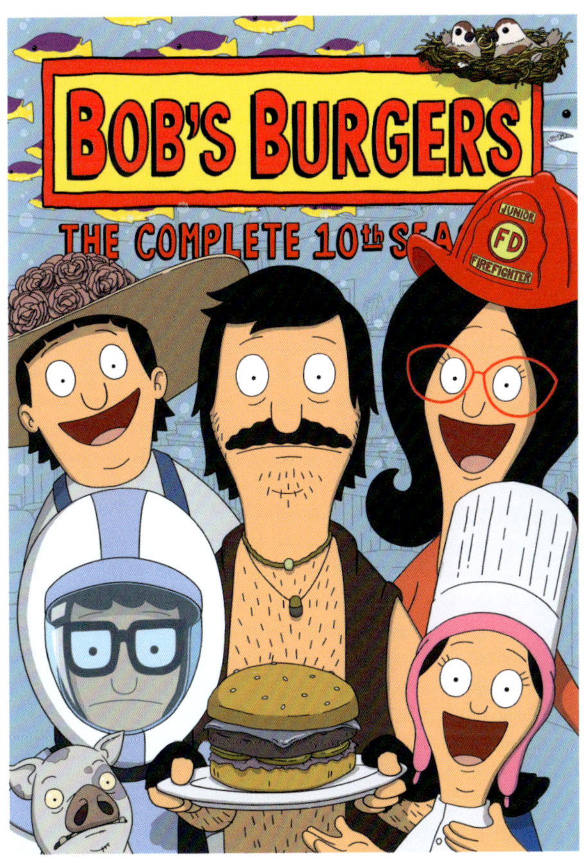

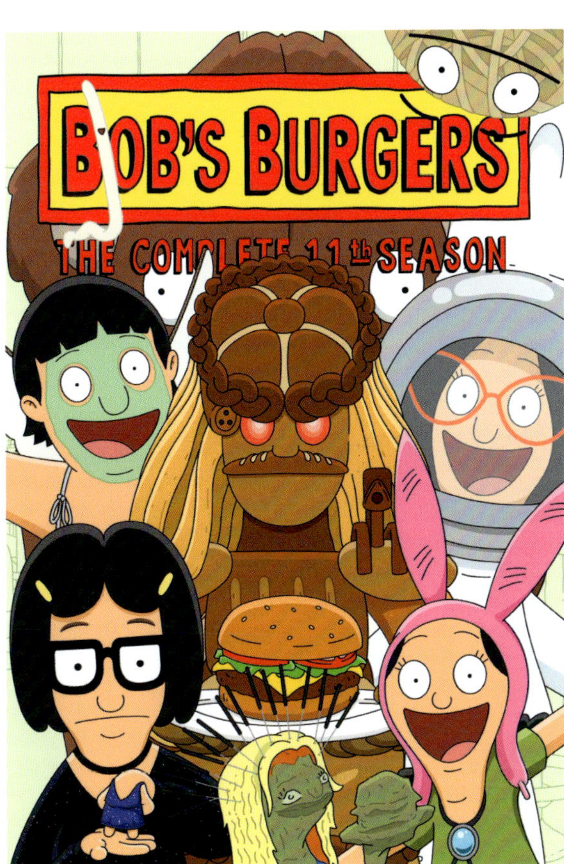

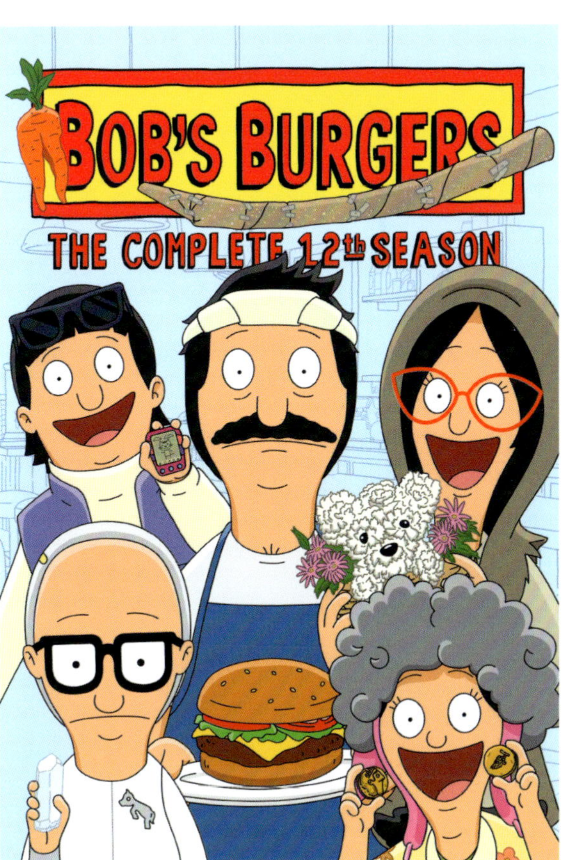

FOLLOWING:

LB: More special art for Comic Con. These were used to "wrap" an entire train! It was pretty exciting for us.

THE MOVIE

LB: To understand the difference between the art of the TV show and the art of the *Bob's* movie, just look at the exterior of the school on the left and compare it to the one on the right. The line is thinner, and an enormous amount of attention has been given to light and shadow, and color temperature, and time of day. On the show, a "stock BG" like this can't be too specific to one time of day or one time of year because we need to reuse it, but in the movie (and in our *My Butt Has a Fever* theatrical short), our production design team, led by Ruben Hickman, went into each background as if it were a singular moment in time, lit by an evanescent glow.

WAGSTAFF
SCHOOL

WAGSTAFF
SCHOOL
TALENT AND/OR PUBLIC DISPLAYS
OF EFFORT CELEBRATION

JIMMY PESTO'S
pizzeria
Yours Truly STATIONERY
HOTEL

BOB'S BURGERS
It's your
FUNERAL
Home & Crematorium
OPEN

CHOKIN

PESTO'S
zzeria
Truly
STATIONER
OPEN
BURGERS

HOTEL

It's your
FUNERAL
Home & Crematorium
BOB'S BURGERS
RETAIL SPACE
AVAILABLE
FOR LEASE

It's your
FUNERAL
Home & Crematorium
BOB'S BURGERS
RETAIL SPACE
AVAILABLE
FOR LEASE

It's your
FUNERAL
Home & Crematorium
BOB'S BURGERS
RETAIL SPACE
AVAILABLE
FOR LEASE

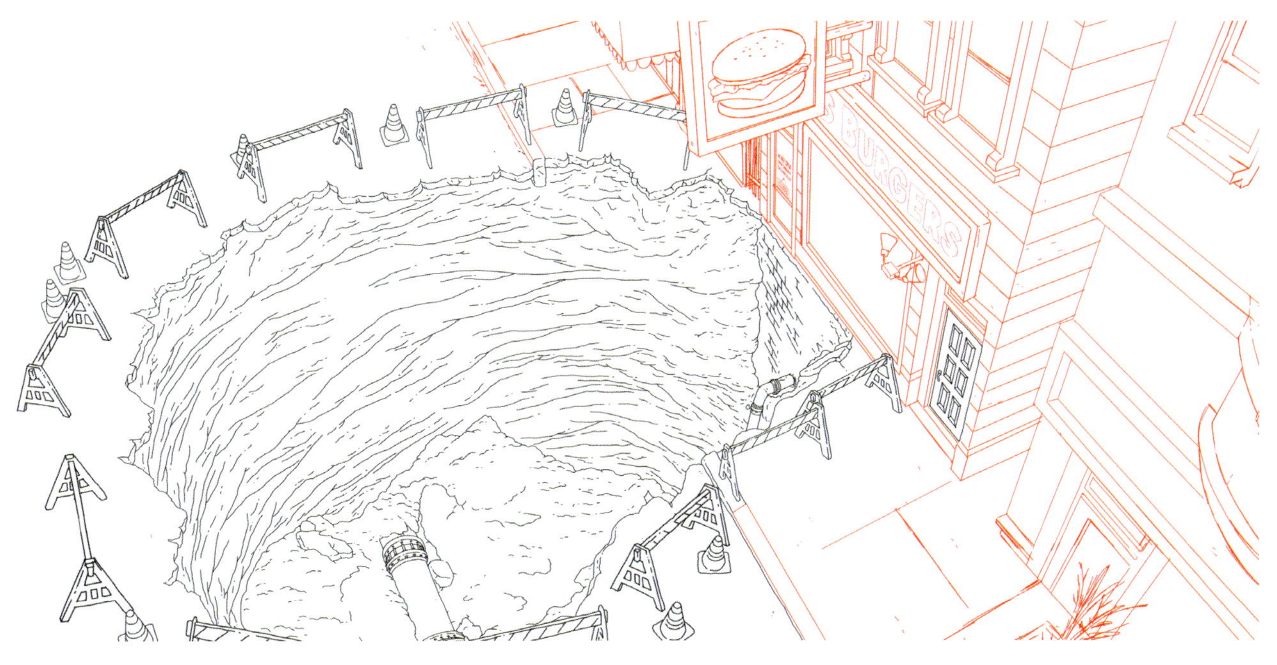

BOB'S BURGERS

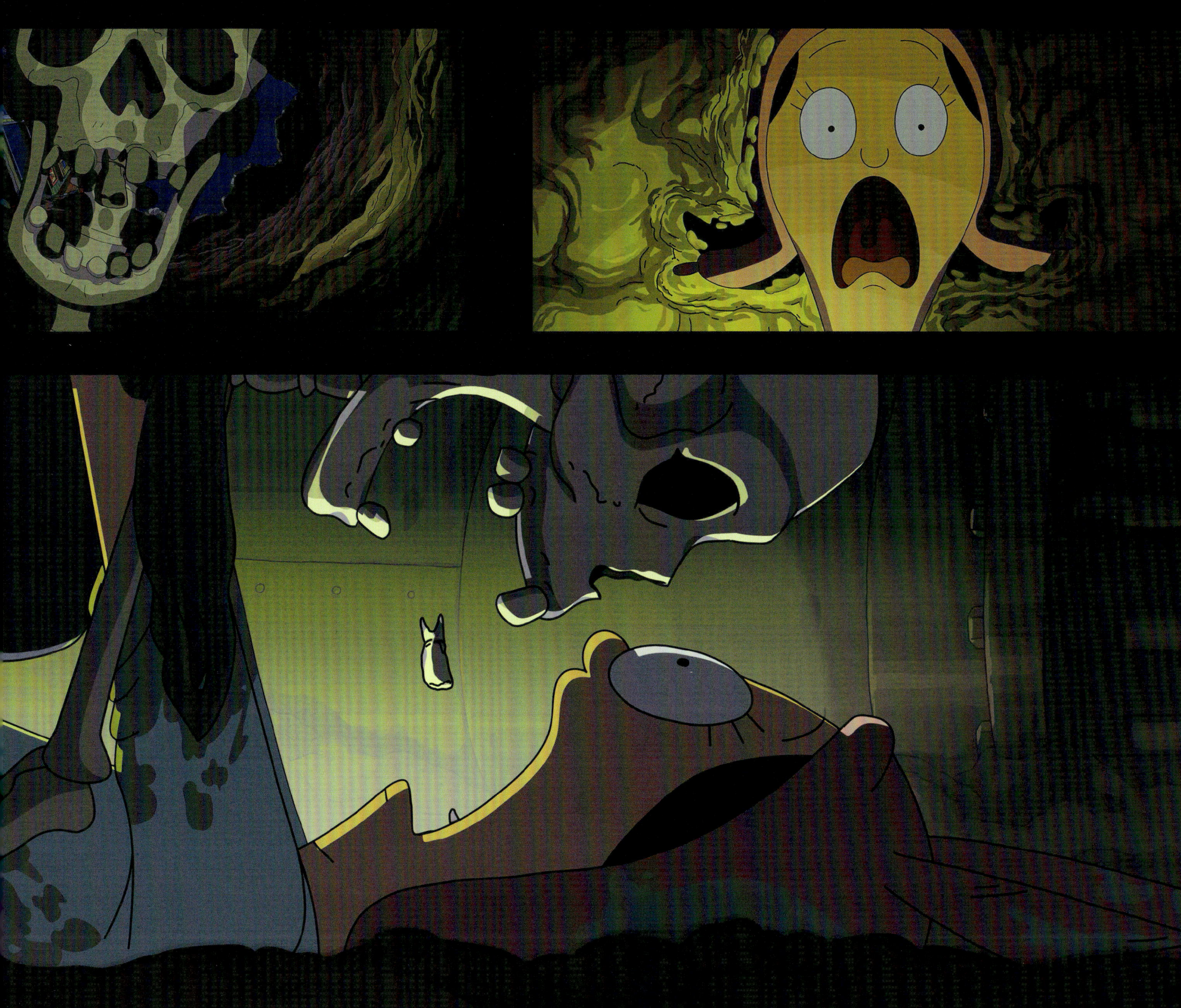

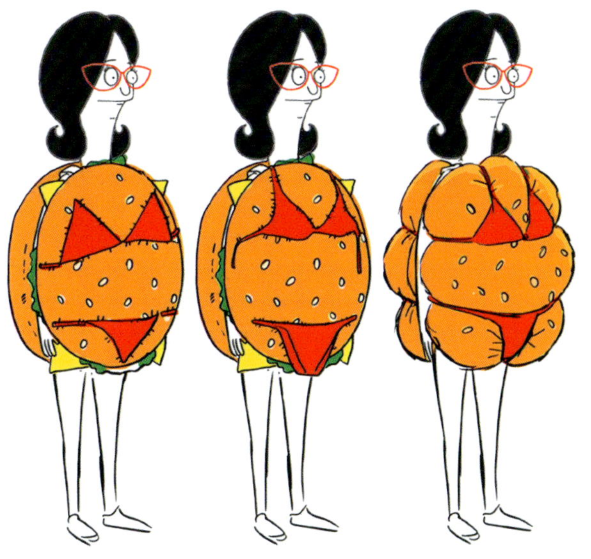

ICKLES

LB: We did a lot of visual development ("viz dev") for the new locations in the movie. Here are sketches and rough paintings of Carniapolis—the hidden trailer park where the Wonder Wharf carnies live.

1
2
3
8
7
4
6
5
A tall guy?
13
14
15
16
17
18
19
20
A Young Don Knotts

ITALIAN & POLISH
SAUSAGE
HOT DOGS

WONDER
WHARF
PARK CLOSED

FUNHOUSE
HOT ICE CREAM
HOT NACHOS
SOUVENIRS

DLE HILL
LOCKER

LB: The hidden space under the pier was another new location. We worked hard to make it believable but also spooky and dangerous.

FOLLOWING (204-207): Some finished art that didn't make the final cut.

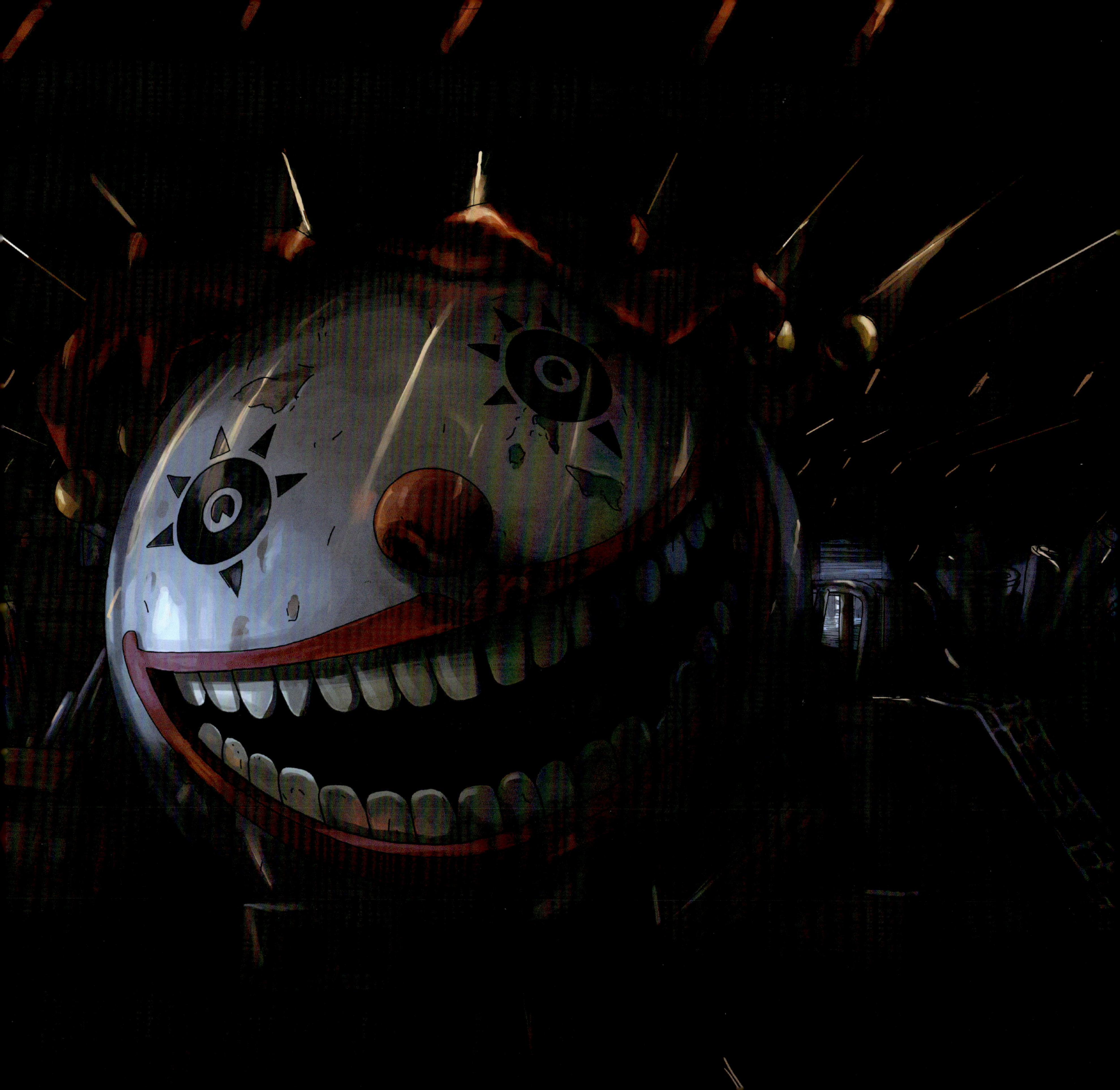

DREAMSVILLE

POSEIDON'S
SEACRET

LB: The heart of the hidden under-pier is the Secret Room. We wanted this to feel like an opulent attraction from a different era—back when these "pleasure piers"(like the ones shown on pages 206-207) were luxurious and fancy and adult.

SHIPS
and
GIGGLES
MOLE HILL

SKY
HAMMER

ICE CREAM
SWEETS

DANGER
BEST BEARD CONTEST
FORTUNES TOLD
LINE STARTS HERE
HOT DOG GUY
POPCORN
YOUR FORTUNE

Scene 040 S38 - Panel 17
Scene 040 S39 - Panel 2

LB: "Viz dev" for Tina's fantasy pop in the opening song. As you probably know, we went with the falling purple petals.

1

MOLE HILL

HOT PIZZA

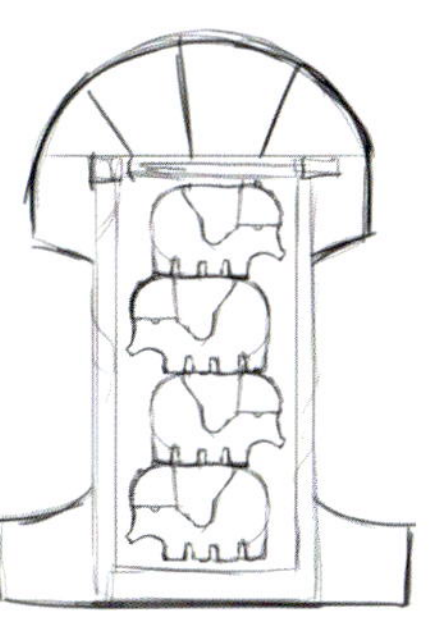

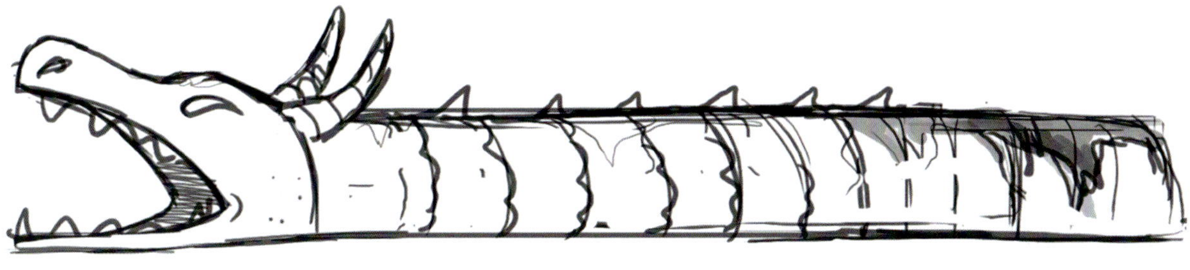

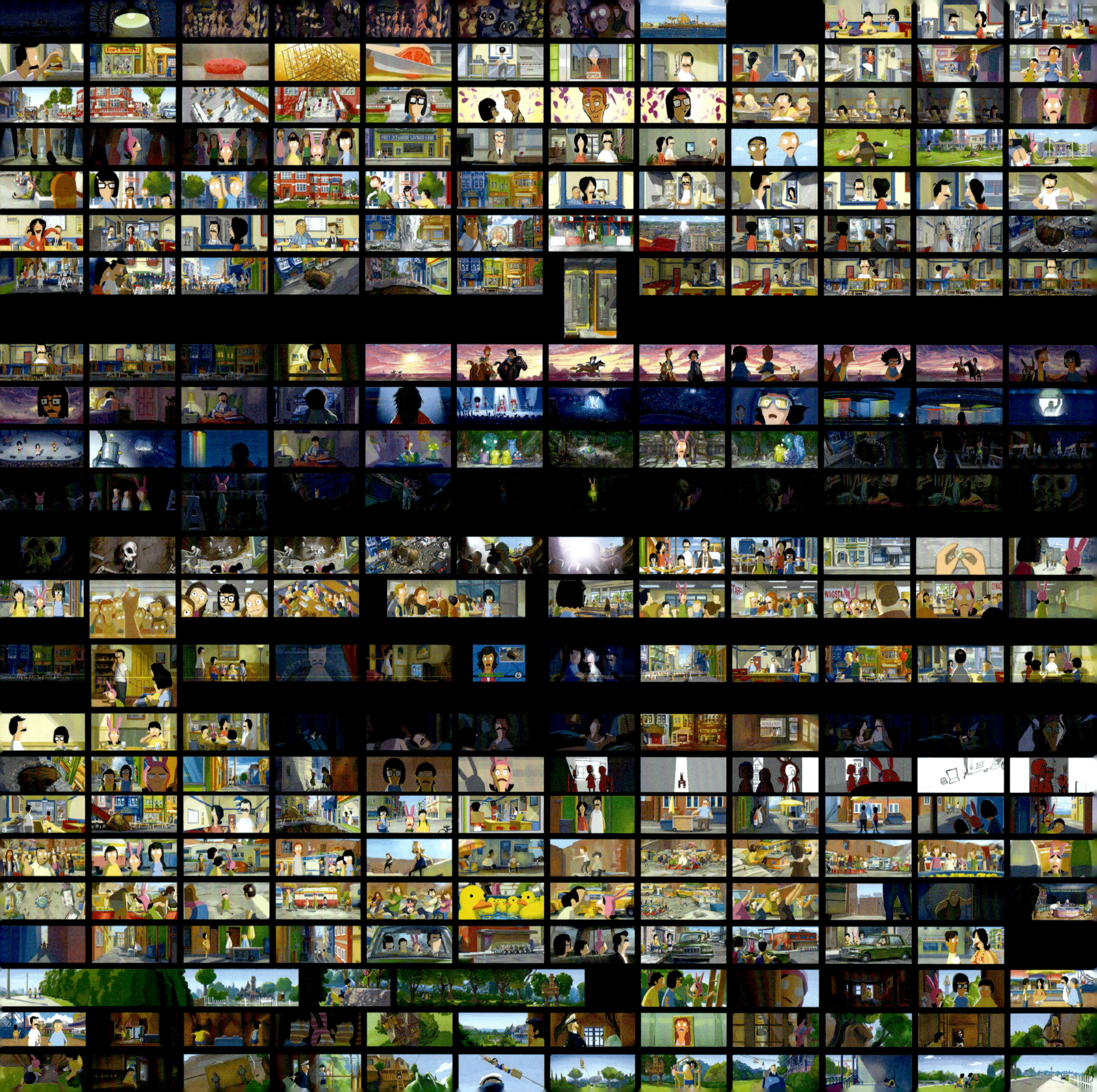

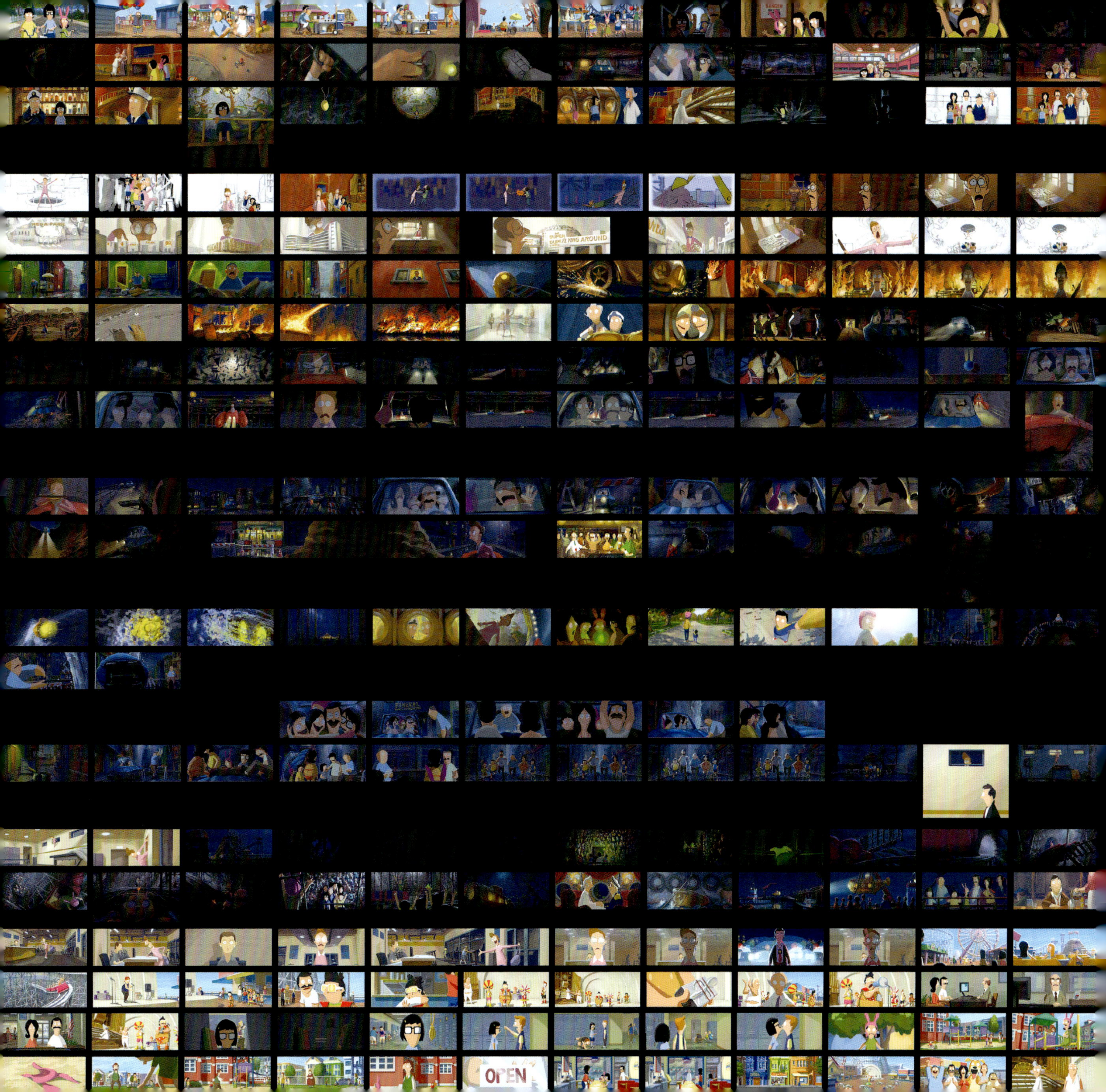

OPEN

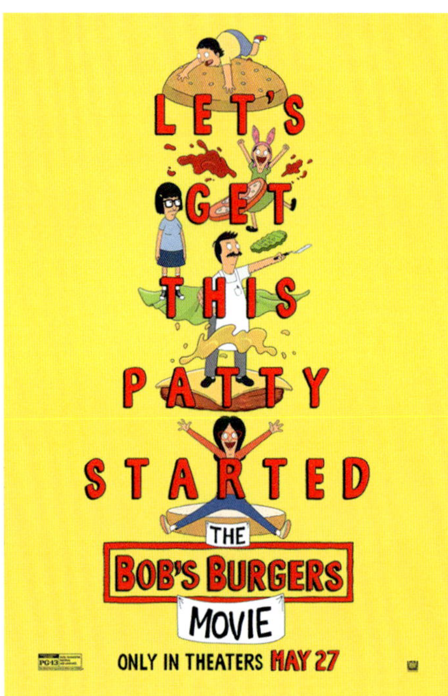

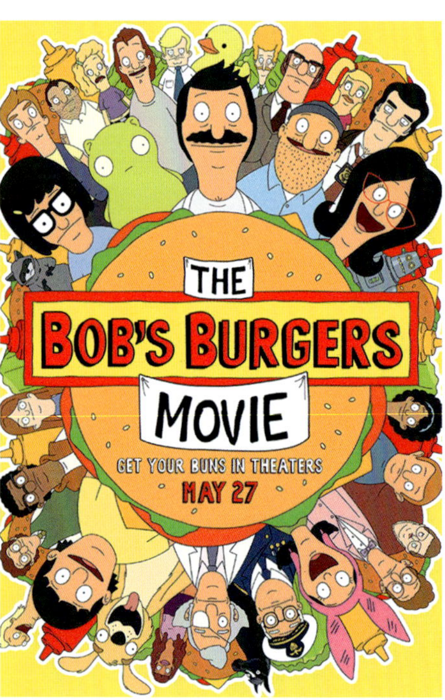

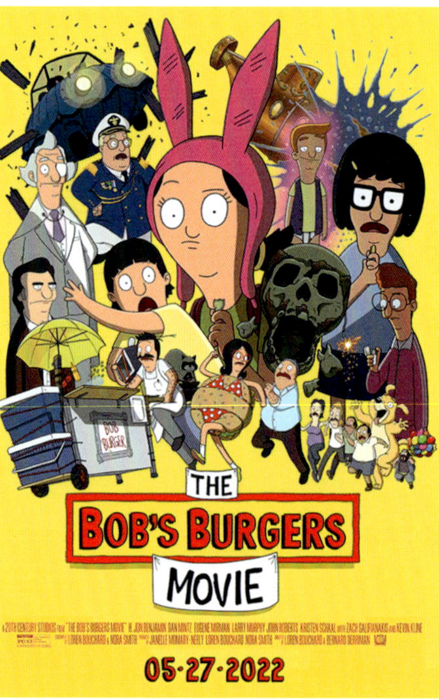

LB: Movie poster design is a whole world unto itself. We wanted ours to feel like a blast of mustard yellow, with the characters jumping out at you, and we wanted the fans to see that burger-suit bikini outfit. And who can blame us?

THE
BOB'S BURGERS
MOVIE

THE
BOB'S BURGERS
MOVIE

THE
BOB'S BURGERS
MOVIE

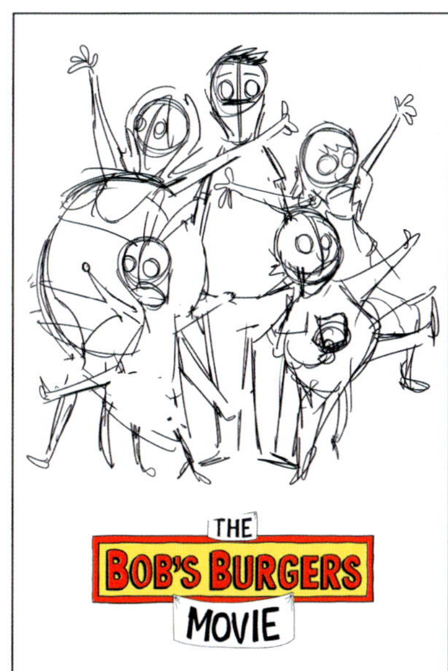

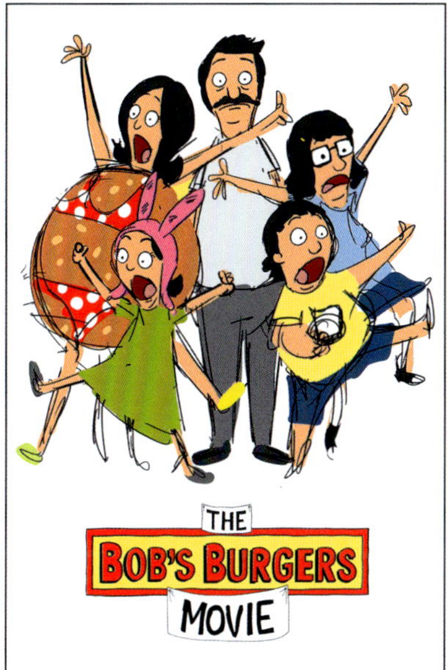

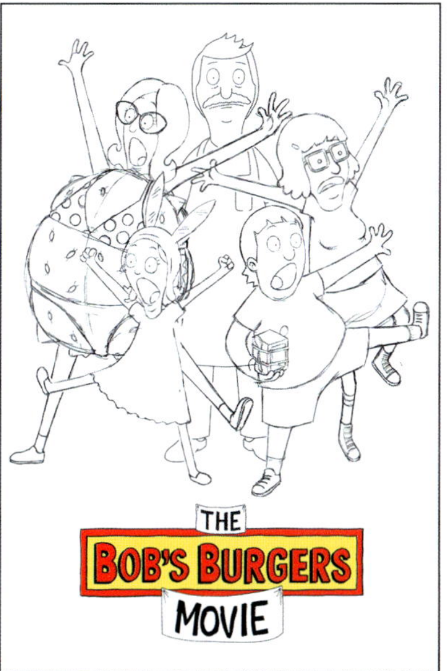

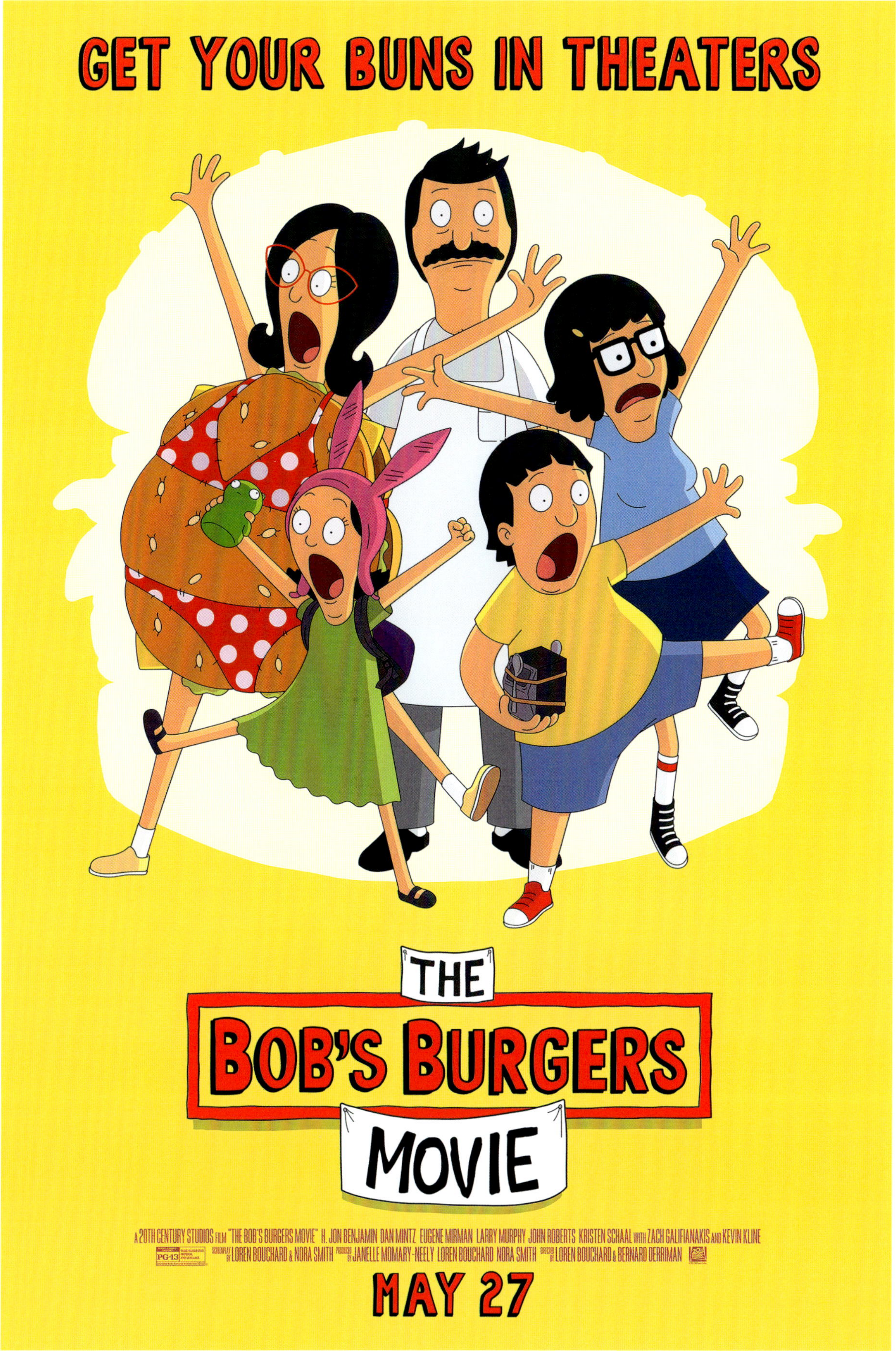
GET YOUR BUNS IN THEATERS
THE
BOB'S BURGERS
MOVIE
A 20TH CENTURY STUDIOS FILM "THE BOB'S BURGERS MOVIE" H. JON BENJAMIN DAN MINTZ EUGENE MIRMAN LARRY MURPHY JOHN ROBERTS KRISTEN SCHAAL WITH ZACH GALIFIANAKIS AND KEVIN KLINE
PG-13
SCREENPLAY BY LOREN BOUCHARD & NORA SMITH PRODUCED BY JANELLE MOMARY-NEELY LOREN BOUCHARD NORA SMITH DIRECTED BY LOREN BOUCHARD & BERNARD DERRIMAN
MAY 27

WONDER
WHARF

CREDITS

2–3: Don Cameron, Walter Mancia, Leah Herskowitz, Ashby Manson, David Merritt
4–5: Phil Hayes, Ben Chuang, Chris Collard
6–9: Jay Howell
10: Jay Howell
11: Sirron Norris
12–13: Jay Howell, Sirron Norris
14–15: Jay Howell
16–17: Jay Howell, Sirron Norris
18: Sirron Norris
19: Dave Creek, Jay Howell, Devin Roth
20: Sirron Norris, Jay Howell
21: Jay Howell
22: Dave Creek, Jay Howell
23: Dave Creek
24–25: Dave Creek, Mike Guerena, Joe Healy, Hector Reynoso
26: Sirron Norris
27: Jay Howell
28–29: Jay Howell
30–31: Dave Creek, Mike Guerena, Joe Healy, Hector Reynoso
32: Jay Howell
33: Jay Howell, Nora Smith
34–35: Dave Creek, Mike Guerena, Joe Healy, Hector Reynoso
36–37: Jay Howell, Sirron Norris
38–39: Dave Creek
40–41: Dave Creek, Mike Guerena, Joe Healy, Hector Reynoso
42–43: Jay Howell
44–45: Jay Howell, Dave Creek,
46–47: Dave Creek, Mike Guerena, Joe Healy, Jay Howell, Hector Reynoso
48–49: Dave Creek
50–51: Dave Creek, Mike Guerena, Joe Healy, Jay Howell, Hector Reynoso, Devin Roth
52–53: Dave Creek
54–55: Dave Creek, Mike Guerena, Garrett Gerberling, Phil Hayes, Phil Lee, Joe Healy, Hector Reynoso
56–57: Bernard Derriman, Phil Hayes, Sirron Norris
58–59: Sirron Norris
60–61: Phil Hayes, Jay Howell, Sirron Norris
62–63: Phil Hayes
64–65: Phil Hayes
66–67: Chad Cooper, Mike Guerena, Scott Moot
68–71: Tony Gennaro
72–73: Dave Creek, Rozalina Touchev
74–75: Liza Epps, Mike Guerena, Scott Moot, Devin Roth, Rozalina Touchev
76–77: Dave Creek, Phil Hayes, Tracy Jones, Hector Reynoso, Yeson Entertainment,
78–79: Mike Guerena, Scott Moot, Kimball Shirley, Rozalina Touchev
80–81: Bernard Derriman, Ed Ghertner, Rozalina Touchev
82: Galina Budkin, Liza Epps, Phil Hayes, Rozalina Touchev
83: Liza Epps, Phil Hayes, Rozalina Touchev
84: Scott Moot, Rozalina Touchev
85: Rudy De La Cruz, Liza Epps, Kimball Shirley, Rozalina Touchev
86: Bernard Derriman, Phil Hayes
87: Tyler Gentry, Phil Hayes
88: Tyler Gentry, Phil Hayes, Scott Moot
89: Bernard Derriman
90–91: Mike Guerena, Phil Hayes, Scott Moot
92–93: Bernard Derriman, Tyree Dillihay, Mike Guerena, Joe Healy, Jose Rodriguez
94–97: Dave Creek, Mike Guerena, Phil Hayes, Joe Healy, Scott Moot, Jose Rodriguez, Derek Schroeder, Kimball Shirley, Yeson Entertainment
98–99: Anthony Aguilando, Tracy Jones, Kimball Shirley, Yeson Entertainment
100–101: Galina Budkin, Dave Creek, Joe Healy, Tracy Jones
102–103: Anthony Aguinaldo, Dave Creek, Mike Guerena, Tracy Jones, Jose Rodriguez
104–105: Dave Creek, Tracy Jones, Rachel Silva, Orlando Velez
106–107: Phil Hayes
108–109: Simon Chong, Phil Hayes, Jose Rodriguez
110–111: Tracy Jones, Britney Lieu, Megan Mathison, Hector Reynoso, Britt Sodersjerna
112–113: Phil Hayes, Tracy Jones, Walter Mancia, Hector Reynoso
114–115: Ben Chuang, Jose Rodrigez, Britt Sodersjerna
116–117: Liza Epps, Kristen Keeves, Cesar Martinez, Cynthia Osaseri, Kat Shea, Rozalina Touchev, Orlando Velez
118–119: Ben Chuang, Mike Guerena, Scott Moot
120–121: Phil Hayes, Jose Rodriguez, Jasmine Wong
122: Phil Hayes, Kimball Shirley
123: Ben Chuang, Kimball Shirley
124: Anna Corrales, Joe Healy, Walter Mancia, Emily Rice
125: Anthony Aguinaldo, Phil Lee, Britney Liu, Emily Rice
126–127: Chad Cooper, Anna Corrales, Garrett Gerberding, Phil Hayes, Britney Liu, Hector Reynoso, Emily Rice
128–129: Mike Guerena, Phil Lee, Scott Moot, Kimball Shirley
130: John Reynolds, Yeson Entertainment
131: Britney Liu, Kimball Shirley
132–133: Dave Creek, Joe Healy, Hector Reynoso, Devin Roth, Orlando Velez
134–135: Anthony Aguinaldo, Chris Collard, Tracy Jones, Kristen Keeves, Hector Reynoso, Emily Rice, John Soto

136–137: Bernard Derriman, Devin Roth, Steve Umbleby
138–139: Bernard Derriman
140–141: Kat Kasmala
142: Emiko Sawanobori
143: Derek Schroeder
144: Maggie Harbaugh
145: Anthony Aguinaldo, Rudy De La Cruz, Jack Herzog, Derek Schroeder
146: Luke Ashworth, Mario D'Anna, J. Forbes, Mike Guerena, Joe Healy, Sara Richard
147: Kaya Dzankich
148: Mario D'Anna, Mike Guerena, Circus Leveo
149: Anthony Aguinaldo, Marcelo Benavides, Tom Connolly, Tony Gennaro, Melissa Jarvis, Travis Millard, Derek Schroeder
150: Dave Creek
151: Bernard Derriman
152: Bernard Derriman, Tony Gennaro
153: Anthony Aguinaldo, Tony Gennaro, Hector Reynoso
154–155: Anthony Aguinaldo, Tony Gennaro, Hector Reynoso, Kimball Shirley
156: Chris Collard, Tony Gennaro
157: Bernard Derriman
158–159: Bernard Derriman, Miranda Dressler
160–163: Bernard Derriman, Ed Ghertner, Phil Hayes, Rozalina Touchev, Yeson Entertainment
164–165: Simon Chong, Bernard Derriman
166–167: Bernard Derriman, Julius Preite
168: Rustam Bekmuradav, Phil Hayes
169: Phil Hayes, Ruben Hickman
170–171: Don Cameron, Ben Chuang, Phil Hayes, Leah Herskowitz, Ruben Hickman, David Merritt, Dennis Venizelos
172–173: Phil Hayes, Leah Herskowitz, Ashby Manson
174–175: Ben Chuang, Leah Herskowitz, Ruben Hickman, Kimball Shirley
176–177: Don Cameron, Phil Hayes, Leah Herskowitz, David Merritt, Katie Rose
178–179: Phil Hayes, Leah Herskowitz
180–181: Bernard Derriman, Mercury Filmworks
182–183: Ben Chuang, Audrey Lai, Britney Liu, Walter Mancia
184–185: Jim Beihold, Leah Herskowitz, Phil Hayes, David Merritt
186–187: Jim Beihold, Ron Catiggay, Ben Chuang, Phil Hayes, Ruben Hickman, Ashby Manson, David Merritt
188–189: Bernard Derriman, Mercury Filmworks
190–191: Ben Chuang, Kimball Shirley
192–193: Ruben Hickman
194–195: Galina Budkin, Ben Chuang, Phil Hayes, Leah Herskowitz
196–197: Bernard Derriman, Britney Liu, Hector Reynoso
198–199: Ron Catiggay, Ashby Manson, Kevin Osorio
200–201: Don Cameron, Ben Chuang
202–203: Jim Beihold, Ron Catiggay, Ruben Hickman
204–205: Ron Catiggay, Ruben Hickman, Audrey Lai
206–207: Jim Beihold, Phil Hayes, Leah Herskowitz, Britney Liu, Jose Rodriguez
208–209: Ron Catiggay Dave Creek, Phil Hayes, Ruben Hickman
210–211: Ron Catiggay, Chris Collard, Bernard Derriman, Phil Hayes, Derek Schroeder
212–213: Don Cameron, Ben Chuang, Phil Hayes, Ruben Hickman, Walter Mancia
214–215: Ron Catiggay, Britney Liu, Kevin Osorio, Dennis Venizelos
216–217: Anthony Aguinaldo, Don Cameron, Bernard Derriman, Ruben Hickman, Britney Liu, Walter Mancia, Hector Reynoso
218–219: Britney Liu
220–221: Phil Hayes, Ruben Hickman, Ashby Manson, Mercury Filmworks
222–223: Phil Hayes, Leah Herskowitz, Ashby Manson
224–225: Don Cameron, Ben Chuang, Leah Herskowitz, Kimball Shirley
226–227: Don Cameron, Ben Chuang, Leah Herskowitz
228–229: Phil Hayes, Leah Herskowitz, Ruben Hickman
230–231: Ruben Hickman
232–233: Ben Chuang, Ruben Hickman, Ashby Manson, David Merritt
234–235: Bernard Derriman, Miranda Dressler
236: Ruben Hickman

Special thanks to everyone who helped to bring all this art to the screen and to the page. As anyone who's ever worked in production knows, behind every stirring image is a team of people who had to shepherd it into existence. And for those of us that are called to shepherding, we know the work is its own reward, but we want to shine a light on these folks regardless:

Nora Smith
Janelle Momary-Neely
Anneliese Glass
Derek McClurg
Christopher Collard
Mary Mancuso
Alex Tritt
Megan Galloway
and Marci Proietto

And at Rizzoli:
Charles Miers
Jessica Fuller
Jacob Lehman

THE
CONTROL

The Rodent
Less Traveled
EXTERMINATORS

FLEA WILLY
PEST CONTROL

DEAD MOUSE SAYS
WHAT
EXTERMINATORS

FLEAS OF BURDEN

RAT TO
REMAIN
SILENT

'SECTS & THE CITY

MOUSE-KA-TEARS

WEEVIL
COMES

SPRAY
IT AIN'T SO

MARE
of FLEAS TOWN

GNAT
MY PROBLEM

RATS WHAT
SHE SAID
EXTERMINATORS

FLIES WIDE SHUT
Exterminators

Bug to Differ
PEST CONTROL

The Mouse
That Jack Kill't
EXTERMINATORS

Done
CONTROL

TERMITE-Y
JOE YOUNG
EXTERMINATORS

DON'T TELL MOM
THE BABY CRITTER'S DEAD
PEST CONTROL

THE WAR ON BUGS
Exterminators

I'D TRAP THAT
EXTERMINATORS

DIE-YOU-MITE!

SQUISH ME BABY
ONE MORE TIME
PEST CONTROL

SEE YA LATER,
FUMIGATOR

MR. VERMIN
CONTROL

YOU BETTER NOT MOUSE,
YOU BETTER NOT FLIES

GNAT SO FAST

PEST SIDE STORY

GONE

IT HAD TO BE GLUE
GLUE TRAP EXTERMINATOR

ONE SQUISH, TWO SQUISH,
RED SQUISH, DEAD SQUISH

IN-GORY-OUS
BUGSTERS

SPIDER OFF DEAD